MERCURY

The astrological anatomy of a planet.

MERCURY

by

Pamela Tyler

THE AQUARIAN PRESS
Wellingborough, Northamptonshire

First published 1985

© PAMELA TYLER 1985

British Library Cataloguing in Publication Data

Tyler, Pamela
  Mercury.
  1.   Mercury (Planet)   2.   Astrology
  I. Title
  133.5'3   BF1724.M4

ISBN 0-85030-325-7

*The Aquarian Press is part of the
Thorsons Publishing Group*

Printed and bound in Great Britain

To Jay Stewart, who had the audacity to assume I could write this in a few years and the Neptunian spirit to keep forgetting *which* years.

Contents

Acknowledgements

Round one of the applause goes to Bruno and Louise Huber, my number one mentors. *Mercury* strays from Huber wisdom in innumerable ways, and for that I accept responsibility. They have nevertheless been the central focus of my own astrological growth, and for that reason I am deeply grateful to them.

Round two of the clapping is for those courageous astrologers who dared wade through the manuscript prior to publication: Geoffrey Cornelius, Andrea Lennon and Teresa Brennan. Many thanks for their salient remarks and constructive criticism.

Round three is for Christopher Hitchings, who did the watercolour of Hermes in Chapter One and the horoscope illustrations.

Last but not least is a special appreciation of those friends and family members who suffered the indignity of my erratic habits this last year: Jane O'Brien, Dianne Falls, Jay Stewart and Stan Shaffer.

Preface

Mercury had its genesis in the fact that astrologers said little about the planet and that it seemed highly improbable that any of them would without sufficient motivation. For an astrologer to bother, it would have to be because Mercury was quite pronounced in his or her own horoscope: I qualified. But having a strong Mercury brings with it problems, such as Mercury's notoriously low threshold for boredom and its difficulty in achieving focus right off the bat. Anything long-winded would really be out of Mercury's league; yet anything too short would really cheat this planet of its rightful significance. How would an entire book ever get written? I debated whether I should write anything astrological for the same reasons that others raise. Who could prove astrology, anyway? And yet I knew intuitively that the argument was debatable — I was just stalling. Thus cornered by my own argument, I set about the homework. I read everything I could find and then still treaded water. Papers got shuffled from one continent to another in some blind hope that *Mercury* might write itself or at least inspire me on some other level. The commitment to put something *on paper* did not come until much later.

My first real glimpse of Mercury came at Christmas 1978, but I didn't know it. I was driving along the Baja Peninsula off the coast of Southern California. To the seasoned traveller, Baja looks much like the rest of the Pacific Southwest: dry, dusty and windswept. Vegetation is nil save for the odd sagebrush (and occasional beer can!). The visit to Baja was made partly out of curiosity and partly as an adventure: neither my friend nor I had ventured far beyond the Mexican border towns. This presented the obvious painless exercise for the motorist, namely to drive from one end of the peninsula to the other. The trip might also have been a game called 'gasoline roulette' or 'Find the petrol': gas was rationed that winter. All too few petrol stations lined the roadway, and fewer still had even heard of unleaded gasoline. The trip south was uneventful except for one indelible impression. Half-way along the peninsula, we came upon a pile of boulders in the shape of a mountain. The map read 'Mt. Pedigrosso'. Someone had obviously been there before and concurred that these were big rocks. Yet my mind was not satisfied by the mere identification of it as Mt. Pedigrosso: first-year geology, second-year geology — I drew a blank. I was unable to account for the boulders; nor was there any immediate evidence that bulldozers had put them there deliberately. Despite an amused co-driver, I found myself marvelling at Mt. Pedigrosso and wondering why it had struck me as so important. What was it? How had it come to exist? The thought of the rock pile stayed with me all the way south. It became a private concern, one I hesitated to share much with a supremely rational *amigo*. Was the mountain really there? Had I missed some other relevant clue?

The ride north came none too soon. For my part, I wanted to quieten the growing obsession. The fact that Mt. Pedigrosso still stood was comforting, although not at all any less puzzling. The mount did, however, mark the half-way point on that day's journey. Months later, the 'rocks' appeared, but in a different guise. An actor friend was doing the play *Bent* in New York and asked me to attend. The play concerns two homosexuals faced with the tedious exercise of moving rocks back and forth between two piles. During this time they are forbidden to communicate with each other. The object of the exercise is, of course, to break the men's spirit, something which never really happens. Ironically, this meaningless and sisyphean task brings them freedom. The rocks, though burdensome, are also a release: they mean survival. Rocks were speaking to me again, but in a different way.

Shortly afterwards, I stumbled across a reference to Mercury/Hermes that brought these two incidents into high profile. Hermes in one of its early Greek translations meant 'He of the stone heap'. Mercury's symbol-making role began to make sense: confronted by the unknown, this god applies labels to the imponderable. Such inventions of the mind appease the immediate discomfort while serving as a reference point for further exploration. Mt. Pedigrosso — the label — had been a useful psychic shorthand. Not until I had made the connection between the impression of those boulders mid-journey and my writing of this book was I able to make any sense of Mt. Pedigrosso's other, more elastic role as symbol. This, then, was Mercury: an elaborate accordion, each key of which bore the note of a particular player.

The chance discovery that Hermes meant 'stone heap' was just the first in a series of incidents too numerous to mention whereby Mercury asserted itself mid-sentence: for example, by presenting me with curious typographical errors such as 'Mercy' for 'Mercury' or by stretching the word 'growing' out by inserting extra spaces between the letters as I typed them. Occasionally, Mercury entertained me with what were outright tricks. The trials of Thoth are case in point. By the middle of 1982 I was unable to ignore the fact that Thoth (Mercury's Egyptian counterpart) wanted a mention in the text. I had toyed with the idea that Thoth might be Mercury's *alter ego* and/or his more noble representative: Hermes evidently thought otherwise. During the Hermes/Thoth debate, Norman O. Brown's book *Hermes the Thief* disappeared. I had turned it over to the reserve desk for safe keeping while I perused the Thoth material. When I returned for it later that day, it was gone. That was most odd — particularly in the light of the British Library's extreme efficiency and the strict rules governing reserve books. It seemed inconceivable to the staff and to me that it had seemingly evaporated. Was Hermes trying to say something?

The trickster motif was familiar terrain and a part of Mercury I wanted to reject — yet here were all the ingredients of divine mischief! It occurred to me that Hermes might have been peeved by his rival Thoth's new-found importance in the book. When the British Library handed me a formal apology for losing *Hermes the Thief,* I noted the time and later asked a horary expert to deal with the question 'Where is the book?'. He agreed, but unfortunately never got round to it before the book turned up again on the shelf the following week. The library staff expressed bewilderment, as they had no idea how it had got there. The fact that the person had not drawn up the map also struck me as significant: granted, he had been ill, but I could not help feeling privately that he might have considered the question trivial (prejudice against Mercury?). The chart raises its own questions about the nature of Mercury in terms of Hermes/Thoth.

Just when Hermes began acting up, Thoth introduced another issue. Geoffrey Cornelius asked me if my work with Thoth had not raised the hackles of Christianity. How right he was, for it was in the middle of the Thoth study that I had become deeply involved in the Anglican Church. I considered dropping astrology and the Mercury contract; I even went so far as to set up my own mini-inquisition! Troubled by the fact that I was a new Christian and still an astrologer, I questioned the vicar and his colleagues point-blank: is astrology intrinsically evil, and, if so, was I therefore in cahoots with Satan? Furthermore, I asked: if astrology is so profoundly off course, how was it that it had brought me to Christ? Were not the Magi astrologers who discovered him via the stars? Their position on astrology was unequivocal: it was unmistakably devilish. (Yet I did not appear to be stricken by Satan.) They could not or would not explain why. My private opinion is that they were expressing Church of England doctrine and holding a separate, unspoken viewpoint. This made sense in the light of what Thoth had taught me about missing pieces: one only looked for them if one knew they were gone. It was obvious that the Church, or at least those Anglicans working with me, refused to acknowledge the apparent discrepancy between astrology's ostensible negativity and the practitioner's capacity to supersede it.

So it was that the most compelling of the epithets given to Thoth had been those related to the 'lost eye'. Thoth's task was clearly detective work, but of a different genre than the sheer curiosity represented by Hermes. Thoth's search was an inward one: a kind of self-imposed investigation concerning the law, both of the spiritual and physical kinds. His journey was also different in that it inspired hope: it bore the virtue of inevitability, the promise of return. For having entered into the process of looking, one had the guarantee of discovery: the lost Moon was certain to come again. The Thoth/damaged eye hypothesis (Mercury-Saturn-Pluto-Virgo) sunk in, as astrological titbits do, on the edge of my consciousness, but I was unprepared to draw any final conclusions publicly. Suddenly it dawned on me that there were actually three males with damaged eyes within my immediate vicinity, and that each one had occupied a special place in my own understanding of the masculine and feminine principles.

Excited by this private 'Ahah!', I passed the observation on to a female astrologer who had the Thoth picture in her chart and whom I knew to be actively working on the masculine/feminine polarity herself. It did not occur to me that she also would bear the physical imprint of Thoth: as it happened, she too was blind in one eye. At about that time I concluded that Thoth spoke through hunches, gut reactions: something I had forsaken throughout the business of writing *about* Mercury. The very issue I carped on and on about in the early chapters — logos — had won. I had been snared by its seductive wiles. Intuition, which had long been my strong suit, had been sacrificed to the god of reason: he had achieved his aim.

The well dried up: I got a classic writer's block and a spate of 'Hurry up!' notices from the publisher. It took Thoth to remind me that I had been conned. Mercury is not *about* anything; it is simply process. Two days before the tête-a-tête with the Church officials I got a solemn reminder: one black eye. Mercury is not usually thought of as Plutonian, although the following lines from *The Visions of Hermes* imply that it just might be. (The phoenix is usually attributed to the sign Scorpio and the planet Pluto.)

'In the same forest I ded see a nest
wherein the two birds of Hermes did lay
One would fly away and the other did keepe him.
And so they — never depart one from the other.

One was of reedd couiller and ye other was white
and both hofe by dying did rise again
more happie and glorious
those birds I have seen to be turned into white doves
and then afterward both have beene changed into one
Phenixe . . .'

The completion of this book brings me full circle. I went to England six years ago to write and do astrology. The return home to America by way of the Christian conversion has another postscript. As transiting Saturn conjoins with my natal Mercury, I enter law school.

Pamela Tyler

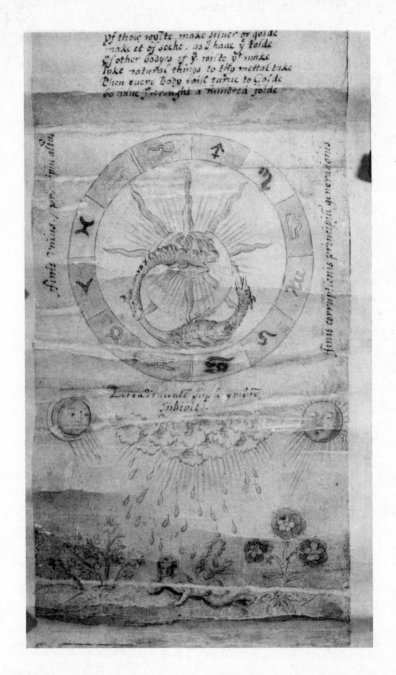

Figure 1 'Zodiac Wheel and Ouroborous' from the Ripley Scrowle.

1.
Bare Beginnings

Begin at the beginning,' the King said, gravely, 'and
go on till you come to the end; then stop.'
Lewis Carroll, *Alice in Wonderland*

Writing about Mercury is no easy task, especially for a woman and
an astrologer steeped in a 2,000-year-old tradition which on the
one hand assigns Mercury the status of neuter and on the other
evaluates it against standards that are decidedly masculine. Part
of the challenge when it comes to tracking this planet is that it never
wears the same outfit twice: it is capable of wearing a dozen different
ones, often simultaneously. In itself Mercury is profoundly neutral
and thus highly impressionable. Its activity is coloured not only
by the socio-cultural bias of the era in question but also by such
influences as gender, regional differences (city vs. country) and
planetary relationships. The resulting overlap between the
environmental factors which exist beyond the horoscope model and
those which exist within it (the planetary aspects, house placements,
structure, etc.) can lead to astrological myopia, a condition in which
the astrologer becomes overwhelmed by conflicting data and is
consequently unable to synthesize the material at hand.

Astrologers typically mistake Mercury's output for its essence,
failing to perceive the fact that Mercury is neither its contents nor
its container. It is, above all, *process.* Process implies movement:
conscious and unconscious, physical and non-physical. It is the
interface between the formidable input-output that Mercury
generates and those external influences which colour its actions.
The obvious difficulty that arises in writing about Mercury is that
one is obliged to write about the very exercise that one is undertaking; forced to stand back and observe those conditions which

facilitate the discovery of Mercury all the while that one is actually
using Mercury in that endeavour. The object of this book is to
encounter Mercury in its obscurity and illuminate its purpose. My
first task will be to consider the tradition from which it springs.

One assumption astrologers frequently make is that Mercury
governs logos or reason, the *sine qua non* of modern civilization.
The error here lies less in ascribing to it the quality of logicality
than in judging it to be exclusively logical and therefore equivalent
to the masculine principle. So far the literature on the subject has
chosen either to beg the question of Mercury's apparently 'sexist'
interpretations or to ignore them altogether. Apart from the cultural
blunder which limits Mercury to the concept of logos, that planet
has to contend with another prejudice, one which is even more
insidious than the first: namely, the astrologer's contempt. No other
planet has been reduced to the level of the outcast of the entire
solar system. Even Saturn, for all its mixed blessings and assorted
reviews, has never been minimalized, yet astrologers regularly lay
the blame for trivialities at the door of exalted Mercury and interpret
it in a superficial, dismissive way. Why does the allegedly 'neuter'
Mercury bear the unmistakable imprint of male chauvinism? And
how is it that astrologers add to the confusion by granting Mercury
the role of logos while in the same breath associating it with business
intrigues and shoptalk? One answer lies in the history of Western
astrology, which since Ptolemy (AD100-170) has developed under
a patriarchical system. The astrologers responsible for most of the
theoretical and interpretive literature still in use today were highly
educated men, and until recently women figured very little in the
intellectual development of the subject. From Ptolemy's day up
to the end of the eighteenth century, astrologers were scientists,
philosophers, mathematicians and theologians, for only those who
were schooled in such disciplines were permitted access to
astrological knowledge. Whatever prejudices our culture has
imposed on the art would seem to have been absorbed by Mercury:
under our predominantly masculine value-system this
impressionable planet has thus acquired virtues that are traditionally
regarded as male.

This raises a separate question: does Mercury assume the burden
of the astrologer's world-view? We know that the environment
influences the way in which Mercury is perceived — does that mean
that an individual astrologer's philosophical outlook therefore
encroaches on his or her perspective of that planet? My guess is
that it does. If, for example, the astrologer perceives the world as

Figure 2   'After a Hermes Head', watercolour by Christopher Hitchings.

'static', then Mercury will be saddled with the burden of a limited or finite view; this planet, like the other nine, will be linked merely with a one-dimensional concept. Similarly, the astrologer who adheres to the principle of duality is bound to be undone by Mercury's witnessing of ten thousand things at once. Alternatively, if the astrologer sees the world as 'moving' or kinetic, Mercury is thereby enriched rather than devalued: a person who identifies with a 'process' motif will bring to their interpretation of Mercury an awareness of life's deeper mysteries. All the same, it is true that many of those who acknowledge a kinetic universe seemingly practise *as if* it were static. This tendency is particularly evident among those astrologers who band together in order to 'prove' astrology. It is the height of absurdity for astrologers to apply causal tests to phenomena which have no known cause: the practising astrologer knows all too well that any attempt to detect a one-to-one relationship between planets in the heavens and occurrences here on earth is doomed to failure. Although the majority of horoscopes might lead one to conclude that there is a close link between the heavens and earthly phenomenona, too many exceptions come to mind where the 'right' interpretation emerged from the 'wrong' chart.

The astrologer's world-view will influence his or her reaction to the last point. Those individuals whose first reaction was 'Ah, 'tis a gullible public they!' would do well to ask themselves if their world-view is not encumbered by a need for tangible evidence that astrology really works; whereas to those of you who nodded your approval of the above, I would say, 'Is not your world-view essentially subjective and thereby consistent with that of a Mercury whose expression is non-linear?' The reader might justifiably ask: why does the question of world-view apply only to Mercury? What makes this planet, as opposed to, say, Mars or perhaps the Moon, carry the onus of one's world-view? Mercury is pivotal because it is the messenger of the ego.[1] It is not the ego itself but the ego's emissary; not the world-view but the representation of it. It acts on behalf of all the other nine planets as a kind of planetary switchboard, a central clearing-house. Each planet influences one's overall outlook, but it is Mercury that is responsible for arranging the final perspective. Its filter reveals whether the chart will have a single, all-encompassing, unifying theme or a divided, discursive one.

In their quest for academic recognition astrologers have stirred up a revolution. Geoffrey Dean's mammoth work *Recent Advances in Natal Astrology*[2] reflects modern astrology's prejudice against itself. Dean's book is a model of one-sided Mercurial excellence: meticulously researched and carefully documented, it is nevertheless woefully remiss in its initial omission of all forms of psychological astrology. Its author's deliberate avoidance of the kind of intuitive astrology that eludes formal testing corresponds to a world-view that degrades the strongly feminine side of Mercury. He attributes the current chaos in astrology to 'the result of chronic infatuation with symbolism at the expense of reason'. Although the book's sequel (unpublished at the time of writing) will introduce the other approach, it is pertinent that the first volume bore signs of the bias of the age. But perhaps this situation is changing. Dean reports that although West Germany's ratio of male to female astrologers is 50:50, only one out of four astrologers in the United Kingdom and America is now male.[3] While females now dominate the astrological population of the West, male practitioners of the art still outnumber their female counterparts in the East. (Hindu astrology's continued emphasis on a 'predictive' approach may be due to the fact that in that culture the astrologer is traditionally male.) The impact of the change in the West from an essentially masculine culture to a feminine one remains open to conjecture, but with luck one might expect a more balanced kind of astrology, and in particular a more balanced understanding of Mercury.

Part of my interest in researching Mercury was to explore the reasons why this planet has posed so many contradictions when it came to interpretation. Thanks to my own volatile Mercury, I found among my clients no shortage of individuals who were overstimulated by its influence.[4] From them I observed that the sex of the person concerned is relevant to an assessment of Mercury's behaviour. Whereas it is fair to say that in charts of both sexes Mars regularly prompted the impulse of assertiveness, Mercury in the same circumstances proved most inconsistent in its behaviour. On some occasions, it would be highly efficient at communicating ego needs; on others, and in an arrangement that was almost identical, it would fail abominably. The distinguishing feature in every case was that of gender. The first clue to Mercury's sex puzzle came when I noted that men and women who had a particularly keen Mercury were often unfocused emotionally. The men would habitually minimize or downgrade the importance of their relationships, yet would go on and on about them — an attitude often accompanied by rather whiny, prudish remarks about not being understood. As for the women, these spoke with a chilling indifference of their

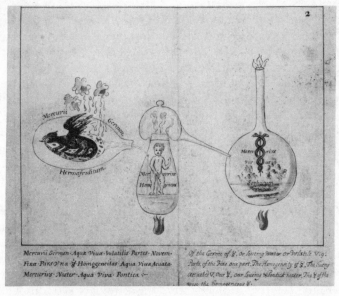

Figure 3 'The Mine of Mercury' (courtesy of the British Library Manuscript Collection).

Figure 4 'Of The Germe of Mercury' (courtesy of the British Library Manuscript Collection).

emotional ties and displayed a curious naïvety where their dependency needs were concerned. Both groups were vaguely giddy about the whole area of important people in their lives — something seemed out of sync. That was when Jung's work on the unconscious suddenly made sense to me. If one is able to conceive of Mercury, as he did, as possessing a dual gender, one can then identify it as the mediator between the conscious and the unconscious:

> 'Son, extract from the ray its shadow and the corruption that arises from the mists which gather about it, befoul it and veil its light; for it is consumed by necessity and by its redness.' [5]

Mercury is both rational and irrational, analogous to the types of activity that are associated with the left and right hemispheres of the brain respectively: the first aligns with the logical, quantitative, abstract function conscious in males and the second with the creative, qualitative, applied function conscious in females. The alliance between Mercury and the unconscious simulates one of the astronomical features that is unique to this planet: From the Earth's perspective, only one side ever *appears* to face the Sun, whilst the other side *appears* to be in a state of nigredo or perpetual darkness, and unobserved. Mariner 10's research on Mercury confirmed that Mercury does expose all aspects of its surface to the Sun; but we, here on earth, cannot see this process. Naked eye observation of Mercury is virtually impossible because of its proximity to the Sun. In addition, Mercury's only sighting position from Earth is such that only one face of Mercury ever shows to us. Thus astronomers, like astrologers require greater than normal effort to apprehend Mercury's significance. If Mercury is taken on face value; it is neither seen nor understood. In essence, one must step outside the ordinary means of observing it in order to know of its full value.

A prominent Mercury in the horoscope of a member of either sex increases the probability of an encounter with the unconscious. According to Jung, the denial of one's internal opposite places the individual most assuredly at its mercy. He calls this state of affairs possession by the anima in the case of a male and by the animus in the case of a woman. Possession by the anima occurs when men become enamoured of the feminine principle, fascinated by feminine characteristics, which they then assume. One sign that this may be happening is the appearance of self-absorption, moods and a rather fussy, old-maidish disposition. Animus possession occurs when women unconsciously identify with the attributes of the masculine principle. Thus the woman who extols too vehemently the power of logos might be in the throes of a full-scale animus possession, of which one of the symptoms is a cold, biting sarcasm, others being a tendency to speak in absolutes and an overconcern for authoritative references. (Emma Jung's book of essays *Animus and Anima*[6] covers this psychic struggle brilliantly.) Gender is a crucial factor when it comes to interpreting Mercury: it dictates the kind of unconscious activity that is probable.

The question of the subject's geographical location further refines the evaluation of his or her Mercury. Urban environments clearly relish Mercury's kinetic mode: they feed on its inherent pleasure in constant change. Mercury functions anywhere but is most attuned to atmospheres of high stimulation. The highly charged Mercurial type living in a sleepy village is bound to be troublesome unless he finds sufficient activity there to sustain his interest; otherwise he will be either perpetually tense or on tranquillizers. (Think, for instance, of a bright child stuck inside a dull classroom — who *really* makes the mischief?) The ideal Mercury space is one where learning is constant and a range of interests is possible. The Mercurial individual caged up in the provinces is the bane of the community, for it is this creature that is most likely to be a chatterbox and ungovernable gossip. The urbanite whose map is markedly non-Mercurial may feel equally trapped; to suggest that such a person might feel rattled by the concrete jungle is to make one step forward in the communication. Chapter 8 will look more closely at Mercury's affinity with the big city.

To recap, we find Mercury responsive to cultural, gender and regional bias as well as to the philosophical stance of its owner/observer. What, then, of the astrology? What internal factors dictate Mercury's unusual importance? Mercury's significance is derived from its role as the *messenger of the ego:* it is not the ego *per se* but the ego's mediator. This distinction is a relevant one, as we shall see when we consider the charts of individuals who allow Mercury 'ego status', men and women who, because of an ego deficiency, value surface behaviour — appearances, etc. — at the expense of their inner autonomy. Such persons are capable of a profound alienation from themselves as well as from the world, their failure to differentiate between inner and outer attributes resulting in an identification with their persona or mask. Mercury is not the persona but the vehicle for numerous personae; not a mask but a series of them applied randomly. When the ego lacks autonomy, Mercury freezes the images it puts across, which then become caricatures of the personality rather than real aspects of it. The persona fixes on a particular mode of being which often proves counterproductive to its true wishes and is invariably self-mocking. The normal ego knows the difference between putting on airs and acting naturally, but the Mercury-ruled ego is not so discriminating. For this reason, Mercury is go-between for the psyche and the world; it is both voice box and resident camera. It is a kind of template on which impressions are grafted: everything has to pass by and through it *en route* elsewhere.

The moment one moves or speaks one makes a statement about the self and the world, one's relationship to it and in it. Mercury betrays every little slip of the psyche, every nudge of the unconscious; it manifests in the tic, the physiological cue that the body proverbially speaks to spite itself. At heart, Mercury is the symbol from which language blooms, the agent of fertility and the bearer of pregnant speech. It is also the master of lost secrets and artful disguise. This gypsy is both a journeyman and an outcast apprentice. With him we equate fire-making and the magic arts: the lore of alchemy is his alone.

Notes

1. Messenger of the gods equals messenger of the ego. Hermes' role as messenger of the gods is analogous to Mercury's role within the horoscope as agent for the competing aspects of the personality's ego, which are, of course, the other planets.
2. Geoffrey Dean, *Recent Advances in Natal Astrology: A Critical Review 1900-1976* (Astrological Association, 1977). An extremely valuable reference work for the research-minded astrologer. Contains good bibliographical material.
3. Dean, *Recent Advances,* p.7.
4. Author bias: Mercury is unquestionably strong in my horoscope, as it makes the only square and tenants an intermediate cusp. A horizontal emphasis (two oppositions along the 1-7 axis) assures multiple contacts with individuals who would gravitate towards someone who shares their temperament.
5. C. G. Jung, *Collected Works* Vol. 14 (Routledge and Kegan Paul, London, 1974) p.99. Jung points out (p.96) that because an alchemical form does not exist in reality, Mercurius must be a projection of the unconscious. He extends this argument by stating that as Mercurius is central to alchemy it must thereby signify the unconscious itself. See also *Collected Works* Vol.

13, p.218, where Jung discusses Mercurius as having a masculine body and a feminine soul.

6. Emma Jung, *Anima and Animus* (Spring Publications, 1969). This is probably the best exposition of Jung's concept of the masculine and feminine principles ever written. Highly recommended.

2.
The Origins of Sweet Deceit

'Tis as easy as lying: govern these ventages with your
fingers and thumb, give it breath with your mouth, and
it will discourse most eloquent music. Look you, these
are the stops.

William Shakespeare, *Hamlet*

Bold-faced lies have never been openly understood or talked about,
mainly because everyone has told at least one in the name of survival.
Part of the enduring significance of lying is that its roots dwell within
the domain of man's earliest activity: the survival of the species.
Prior to conquering and controlling territory, man was obliged to
manipulate his surroundings in order to obtain food, shelter and
warmth. Eventually, through a process of trial and error, he devised
a similar process for protecting his own property. Yet first he needed
a means of communicating with the environment. Grunts gave
way to language, which classified and ordered man's universe and
provided him with a vehicle for the exchange of information; it
also afforded concepts of identity and possession, such as 'me' and
'mine'. Primitive man, like a nine-month-old baby perceived the
world as an extension of himself. The objects seized were violently
guarded from potential intruders. No one faults the primitive's
strategies for safeguarding his possessions: within the context of
survival, deception and camouflage are both prudent and
reasonable.

Mercury's reputation as the original cattle thief stems from his
early Greek role as Hermes, protector of the shepherd from thieves.
The institution of cattle raiding in ancient Arcadia (Hermes'
legendary home) allowed robbery provided it was done openly and
with force. [1] The Festival of Hermes at nearby Samos gave people

general licence to steal once a year. Theft, or the appropriation of goods in secret was however never sanctioned.

Hermes' job was to detect and outsmart the cunning rustlers who stole cattle by stealth. He was particularly able in this task because he could observe the thieves while remaining invisible. Gradually, the line between robbery and theft blurred in conjunction with the rise of 'silent trade' or legitimate thieving. This latter practice involved an exchange of goods between buyer and seller at a site sacred to Hermes. A seller would leave his wares at the stone monuments and then depart. The buyer would arrive later and *take* whatever was there leaving some token in return. Thus, Hermes as guard against thieves became their patron. Norman O. Brown accordingly dubs him 'Patron of stealthy action'.[1]

Just as children readily confess an affinity with the robbers in 'cops and robbers' TV serials, so too do adults betray a psychic weakness for the clever con. Our appreciation of the bad guy in the good/bad guy saga is measured by something else: generally our opinion of just how clever, witty or original he was in effecting his getaway.

Mercury's slippage back and forth from one side of the law to the other explains the fuzzy boundary found between the best crooks and criminologists. Both get kudos for being shrewd; both cherish the privilege of working incognito. Mythology illustrates the close alliance between law and outlaw in the tale of Hermes and Apollo.

Hermes, Maia's new-born son, ventures forth in his swaddling clothes on the first day of his life to rob his brother Apollo of his oxen. In order to escape detection he ties giant sandals backwards on the oxen's hooves and leads them in the opposite direction. By sunset he has returned to his crib, all innocence and smiles. Apollo susses out his baby brother's indiscretions and takes him to Olympus where their father Zeus extracts a confession from him and enquires about the method of theft. Amused by his wayward son's ingenuity, Zeus first chastises him and then persuades Apollo to continue dealing with him; he also assigns to him various tasks related to social finesse. Hermes is appointed Messenger of the Gods and entrusted with the duties of making treaties, promoting commerce and maintaining the rights of travellers. Zeus gives him a herald's staff with white ribbons (sometimes shown as snakes) which can cast spells, decipher dreams as well as make himself invisible. Hermes' snake entwisted wand, known as a caduceus, could also heal people and put them to sleep. For this reason, the caduceus has come to symbolize the medical profession. In addition, Zeus presents Hermes with the gift of flight in the form of golden-winged sandals. The need for quick escape and incessant travel consequently permeates the Hermes ethic. We find it is also Hermes who assists the Fates in the composition of the alphabet and the musical scale and the invention of astronomy; he even teaches the Olympians the art of making fire.

Annoyed by their father's apparent admiration for the child thief, Apollo returns his oxen minus one to the valley. Meanwhile, inventive Hermes fashions from the remaining cow gut and a tortoise's shell a delicate musical instrument on which he sings Apollo a song of praise. Seduced by this lyre, Apollo offers up his remaining cattle in exchange for it. Hermes agrees, provided Apollo

Figure 5   Hermes with a lyre, taken from a fifth-century vase.

instructs him in augury and divination. The latter refuses, sending Hermes instead to the Muses, from whom he acquires the art of pebble reading.

Certain points in the myth deserve elaboration, and while some of them will be treated here, others will be dealt with in ensuing chapters. The story tells us that on the first day of his life Hermes stole from his brother, displaying that infantile greed which makes no distinction between the self and others and which causes the objects of desire to be seized or devoured. This urge for contact is first observed when the baby suckles the mother's breast. In this instance the relationship between mother and child is an ambiguous one. Maia's cave existence suggests a mother who is subordinate and whose image is diffuse. She appears aloof and separate, and the interaction is negligible. The social clouds that surrounded Hermes' birth further complicate the nature of their bond. Brought into the world as the result of Zeus' tryst with this lowly nymph, Hermes is thus born with sub-Olympian status. The fact of being the product of indiscriminate coupling injures his pride. Whether he rejects his mother or is rejected by her is unclear; but what is certain is that his first encounter with the world is an aggressive one. There, driven by insecurity and jealousy, he challenges his half-brother, Apollo. In psychological terms, what is implied is that premature weaning caused by either the infant's or parent's decision results in uncivilized behaviour; studies of the background of juvenile delinquents reveal that antisocial conduct can be traced to a feeling of rejection by the mother.

While it was originally believed that early feeding patterns dictated an infant's later emotional development, research carried out on animals has shown that the quality of contact is more important than the actual provision of food. Harlow's monkey experiments[2] illuminate this point. The experimenters built two 'mothers', one of wire and the other of soft terry towelling. They bore no resemblance to monkeys, although they were shaped into heads and torsos. Only one of these 'mothers', the wire one, was fitted with a device that enabled young monkeys to obtain milk by sucking. The goal of the experiment was to see whether the 'mother' that was also a source of food would be the only one to which the young monkeys would cling. The results were straightforward: the infants chose the cuddly cloth version as opposed to the more reliable, milk-dispensing wire model.

The nature of the attachment is a function of the mother's responsiveness to the baby's needs. While most babies show *secure attachment* to the mother, some display what is known as *anxious attachment*. [3] This condition is seen in babies that show avoidant or ambivalent behaviour when at first separated from the mother and then reunited with her. This defence mechanism seemingly arises from the anxiety that occurs when the mother is someone who cannot be depended upon consistently. This represents a mild form of the more extreme detachment characteristic of children who have experienced a prolonged separation from their parents; such children show indifference to their parents when first reunited with them. [4] In the legend, Maia's support is weak: her nurturing appears inconsistent, and there are no signs of physical contact, such as fondling or cuddling. Hermes' action on day one — symbolically equivalent to the first year of life — is not merely that of a frightfully precocious *enfant terrible* but also that of a desperately needy child seeking contact and love. What is expressed here is the feeling of restlessness, a sense that he should find some justification for his existence. The means he employs are those of wit and barter.

In real life, the Mercurial type wavers between a cynical, detached attitude towards the family and a sentimental, even soppy feeling where such things as special holidays and birthdays are concerned. Both sexes express ambivalence towards the mother. The biological mother, like Maia, remains in the background, her image vague and undifferentiated. She appears in very low profile, often playing a backseat role to a somewhat formidable, tyrannical husband/father/Zeus figure. For women, this means a fairly long, protracted struggle with the issues connected with femininity, possibly involving a rejection of the role of giving birth. Relationships with men become imbued with power images, such as those attributed to the Olympian king, Zeus. Men showing pronounced Mercury traits will share the Mercurial woman's uncertainty towards the mother, but in this instance the quality that will be assigned to her is a deep, mysterious power. A lack of close contact with the exalted father leads such men to wrestle uncomfortably with members of their own sex. The net result for both groups is firstly an erotic complication, a difficulty in establishing close emotional bonds due to the mother's actual indifference to her own role as provider of warmth and security, and secondly, an impermanence of activity, an incapacity to sustain continued involvement in any project because of an exaggerated fear of failure to meet the father's Olympian standards.

'Rich man, poor man, beggarman, *thief,* doctor, lawyer, Indian chief,' goes the child's rhyme. The first part of the Hermes-Apollo tale considers the instinctive thieving of the insecure primitive being, whilst the second depicts Hermes' fast-developing ability to rationalize his deviant behaviour. This achievement represents a step up on the individuation scale, albeit not a very big one. Astrologers have long sought to demonstrate the degree of an individual's honesty from his or her horoscope. In his formidable *Dictionary of Medical Science* Cornell lists liars or falsifiers as holding Mercury afflictions at birth.[5] Like Firmicus Maternus in *Ancient Astrology: Theory and Practice,* Cardan and others, he attributes Mars and Saturn ties to Mercury as indicators of native dishonesty, but with regard to such link-ups it would perhaps be more accurate to say that issues of honesty surface for the individual in question. Consider Immanuel Kant's view on the subject of lying.

> Truthfulness in statements which cannot be avoided is the formal duty of an individual to everyone, however great may be the disadvantage accruing to himself or another.

Yet Kant's own horoscope reveals aspects that are traditionally associated with inherent dishonesty. Mercury and the Moon form conjunctions in Aries in the first house, squaring Saturn in Capricorn and Mars in Cancer, and Neptune, while unafflicted in the sense that it forms no hard aspects (square, opposition, conjunction), nevertheless sits in the third house, with Venus. (One wonders what conclusions the ancients would have drawn about the character of this German philosopher whose interest in ethics and aesthetics dominated a lifetime!) It seems that in Kant's case the tendency towards dishonesty was projected in the form of an attack on lying.

Modern astrologers add Mercury aspects to Uranus, Neptune, and Pluto as clues to deceit. However, from my experience, 'deceit' in the horoscope relates more directly to the native's relative ego strength (Sun, Moon and Saturn), mutability, and elemental emphasis. How far any one chart lifts itself beyond the lure of the trickster is a matter of individual consciousness; at the present time, the determining of consciousness from the horoscope is beyond the parameters of astrology. Deception, like people, differs in degree and kind.

The inclination to invent stories aligns itself with personality disposition. One way of classifying 'lies' is to set them in the broad framework of the astrological elements: fire, air, water and earth. Each element describes a particular way of relating to the universe and, by extension, one's habitual defence pattern.

Fire Lies

Fire liars put giant sandals on cattle hooves: they bluff. Purveyors of fishing stories and blarney, they thrive on the spectacular. Part of the lying is for fun, while some of it feeds the ego. Self-aggrandizement, bragging, pontificating and so on are all part of the fiery repertoire. The truth is coloured by romance, inspiration, creativity. Their yarns smack of *Don Quixote;* their locker-room stories get laughs. The whole encounter with a fire lie is at once theatrical and adventuresome, the fashion in which the deception is carried out accounting for nine-tenths of its success. This variety of falsehood is the most easily recognized and the most socially indulged, because although everyone knows that the minnow was, no one really cares. Breaking the spell of a fire tale is taboo; the extravagance of expression is so contagious that it escapes censure. The force of make-believe is such that audiences applaud it.

The ones who are the most vulnerable to the fantastic are the earthy types: they take everything so literally that it does not occur to them that they have been sold down the river. The fiery type is equally susceptible to someone else's hyperbole; it is a salesman's *bête noire* that he or she is renowned for being the world's biggest sucker. Aquinas would probably have listed this form of lying under 'jocose' (told in jest) meaning that he, like most other people, would not consider it to be the most morally reprehensible.

Water Lies

Water lies are those uttered for the purpose of saving face: they protect rather than expand the ego. Hermes' denial of misconduct before Apollo typifies watery evasion. Deceit occurs in the form of half-truths or lies of omission, denial by silence being a popular method. The secretive personality of water signs accounts partly for this. Also typical is the tendency to malinger or to evoke sympathy for one's imaginary illnesses. Water's hysterical edge means that it can exaggerate a bit; like fire, it embroiders or muddies the facts. An element of absent-mindedness contributes to its apparent subterfuge, and self-deception, usually unconscious, is common.

Water liars get so caught up in their own fictions that they start believing their own stories, for watery personalities kid themselves about personal motivation. Air types are naturally attracted to water's subtle maneouvring, and these two groups half-collude in order to keep conditions cool and unruffled. Water and air manufacture images, personas, their joint distortions being for the most part connected to roles, to interpersonal relationships. In both instances the orientation is towards harmony and the smoothing over of rough edges. Sissela Bok describes this kind of fabrication as essentially paternalistic,[8] that is, the individual may justify his or her actions by citing benevolent reasons. Bok points out that this form of altruism is more likely to be indicative of a fear of confrontation, a need for change: in other words, it masquerades as being designed to help others but in reality merely helps the person concerned.

Earth Lies

By the standards of many people, earth falsehoods are the only *real* lies: they represent a clear obstruction of the truth. These generally accompany the seizure of property. Earthy individuals do not fib; they perjure themselves. They do not just bamboozle; they plot, premeditation being the key. Earth's assault on the truth attains Machiavellian proportions. The motivation for earth lies rarely includes self-aggrandizement, the purpose being rather the saving of one's own hide. Because earth signs tend towards concrete, practical interests their mendacity usually involves very few loose ends: their stories are airtight and any alibis made are clear-cut. (The need to embellish or overstate the case falls to earth's opposite element, fire.) Earth frauds arouse the largest amount of social criticism, for they constitute broken promises and major breaches of faith. Typical of this category is the frame-up, whereby another individual is deliberately placed in a compromising position. Also familiar with reference to this temperament are the extortionist and the blackmailer: the motive is material.

Dante's *Inferno* ranks this form of lying as just above treason. The eighth circle of hell contains those souls guilty of crimes found uniquely among men.[9]

Air Lies

The air con is the subtlest of them all. Social rituals demand them, and diplomatic circles breed them. White lies are the easiest to commit because their goal of peace-keeping is morally justifiable: air ruses masquerade as social etiquette. Here, pretence hides insincerity. Another airy tactic is mental intimidation, the difficulty being that it is usually carried out with a high degree of finesse. This form of hoodwinking is the most refined and invidious of all; persuasive tongue-twisting and pedantic sophistry form the basis of the intellectual dodge. Watery people are the ones who are most vulnerable to airy half-truths, for the reason these subjects are easily seduced by words. Heavyweight rationalization is the weapon of the air brigade; like fire forms, air dramas are socially forgiven, though for quite different reasons. A blend of airy double talk and earth's insistence on concrete evidence breeds the cumbersome egghead.

Double talk, whatever its purpose, is the tool of air. Newspeak, the special language George Orwell wrote of in his book *1984,* shows how. In the story, the decision to eliminate large categories of vocabulary was made under the pretext of economizing speech; in reality, this abridging of vocabulary resulted in the limited expression of thought — in other words, mind control. Orwell's birth time is unknown, so we cannot evaluate his entire chart, but what is striking from the data listing below is his grand trine in air (Mercury-Mars-Saturn). Mercury is, appropriately, stationed in its Huber strong degree of eleven Gemini.

George Orwell, June 25, 1903, Motihari, India, 11.30 a.m. LMT (speculative)

Sun 2 Cancer 30	Moon 2 Cancer 18
Mercury 11 Gemini 01	Venus 17 Leo 17
Mars 8 Libra 25	Jupiter 22 Pisces 44
Saturn 8 Aquarius 20 rx	Uranus 23 Sagittarius 16 rx
Neptune 3 Cancer 23	Pluto 19 Gemini 30

Table 1 Horoscope data for George Orwell (Lois Rodden, *The American Book of Charts*).

A preference for one brand of duplicity as opposed to another is a bit like soap powder commercials: you can dress up the cartons in a dozen different ways, but at the end of the wash the clothes just *have to* come clean! The dominant element in a horoscope may be found by using a proportional weighing scale for the personal points and planets. However, this can occasionally be misleading. Elements showing a void sometimes have more power than those registering the highest points; thus Beethoven, for example, with his ostensible 'lack of water', emerges as one of the musical geniuses renowned for their deep emotive power. To complicate matters, planetary aspects can override elemental balances. Although I have reservations as far as precise, one-to-one correspondences between planets, signs and houses are concerned, I admit that it can be useful to acknowledge any similarities that exist. If, after you have considered the various elements and aspects, no particular element seems to shine through, return to the Sun sign, the rationale for this being that the Sun's position is the focus of the ego and it will be the final arbiter of Mercury's action.

The charts selected for this chapter illustrate two kinds of Mercurial shenanigans. The first example falls into the category of fire/earth/water fraud: the motive for it was purely material and it involved outright stealing. The second is more subtle. It,

Figure 6   Hermes Kriophorus (Collection Piot).

too, represents fraudulent activity, the difference here being that the air component combines with water, lending an altogether gentler approach to the bogus operation in question. The first is a joint effort; the second the work of an individual. Hailed as the crime of the century, the Great Train Robbery has a horoscope which is a brilliant demonstration of Mercury's thieving disposition. On August 8, 1963, fifteen experienced con men masterminded the robbery of over two and a half million pounds.[12] The method they used was fittingly Mercurial: that of tampering with the railway switches in order to stop the train between stations. The fact that this robbery took place within a key Mercury environment — transportation — makes its story all the more compelling for astrologers. Though engineered by professionals, it nevertheless proved to be a bungled operation.

A sneak preview of Mercury's position taken before tackling the entire chart confirms our expectations. The planet *is* strong here: not only is it located in its own house and sign (the third house and Virgo), but it also forms conjunctions with Uranus and Pluto, often deemed Mercury's higher octaves. These two planets share Mercury's relationship to the thought process, amplifying its obsessiveness, its inventiveness and its tendency towards erratic behaviour; more importantly they contribute to its inherently antisocial streak. Gemini's twelfth house cusp position informs us that Mercury's work will have a largely secretive, behind-the-scenes function. The triple conjunction of Mercury-Uranus-Pluto underlies the careful pre-planning undertaken by the train robbers. Pluto seems to be involved with the original detective work done by the group in tracking the actual movements of the high-value mailbags. Uranus injects chutzpah into the carrying out of the big heist; it also brings carelessness in covering over incriminating evidence.

Recalling that Mercury's function is that of spokesman for the rest of the planets, in particular the Sun, let us examine the arena in which our excitable messenger did his bit. Most of the planets fall within the first quadrant (the first, second and third houses), suggesting a preoccupation with material survival. The strong eastern hemisphere intimates a rather egocentric view of the world, one that is expressed by the familiar saying, 'Every man for himself'. This attitude probably accounts for the fact that the team effort failed; the robbers eventually began stealing from one another. Left-sided charts show that co-operation is resisted and that there is a need to do things alone. Moreover, the suspicious, distrustful streak that characterizes eastern charts forces such individuals to

Figure 7   The horoscope chart of the Great Train Robbery.

negotiate their own successes: each of the train robbers performed a specific task and each orchestrated his own escape route.

The aspect direction, which is either vertical or horizontal, reveals the degree of contradiction of purpose. Although some of the aspects here rise from the base of the chart towards the MC, implying social ambition, the bulk of them straddle the lower part of it, suggesting an exaggerated adherence to family tradition. Charts of this order show those who absorb wholeheartedly the messages of their community and for whom peer-group values play an extremely significant role in their later development. Thus the Great Train Robbery's chart might be taken to symbolize the ethic, heritage and orientation of the robber. Like Hermes' somewhat dubious origins, the train robbers' birthright could hardly be said to have initiated them into Olympian status. E. J. Hobsbawm's remarks on the nature of bandits seem appropriate here:

> The crucial fact about the bandit's social situation is its ambiguity. He is an outsider and a rebel, a poor man who refuses to accept the normal rules of poverty and establishes his freedom by means of the only resources within the reach of the poor, strength, bravery, cunning and determination. This draws him close to the poor, he is one of them. It sets him in opposition to the hierarchy of power, wealth and influence: he is not one of them. [13]

Against the background of a tough South London neighbourhood where violence plays a routine role in family and street life, social mobility is defined by money. Getting freedom means scaling the ladder of crime, in this case by graduating from such things as one-off TV thefts to full-scale rail high jinks.

Two other important features colour the robbery's map: Cancer rises, and its ruler, the Moon, is located in Pisces on the midheaven. The Moon's position ensures high visibility for the group involved as well as public sympathy. Their reputation is enhanced by elements of imagination and deception; the public hold the incident in high esteem because it feeds part of their own fantasies. Taken as the horoscope of the train robbers themselves, this midheaven position describes their wish to attain a dream sum, in this case over two million pounds. The event chart is further electrified by Venus' extravagant placement in Leo on the second cusp. Money is usually assigned to the second and eighth houses, and Venus is the natural second house ruler: a desire for vast amounts of money is quite in keeping with the Leonine sense of proportion! Leo's attitude of childlike gamesmanship is also suited to the grand-scale version of cops and robbers. Those train robbers who were not caught by the police found themselves running rapidly out of cash because of their careless, self-indulgent spending.

Given the contrast between Sun-Saturn-Neptune's image as victim/victimizer and Venus in Leo's bold, ostentatious streak, this chart sheds a great deal of light on the nature of the conflict-organizing thieves themselves. There is a conscious or unconscious resentment concerning the social distribution of wealth and an immature, impetuous side that seeks immediate gratification. The train robbers were clearly aggressive types, but more passive personalities holding this Sun-Saturn-Neptune T-square might underestimate their self-worth, becoming vulnerable to job exploitation. (An extreme case of this would be those captured for the slave trade.) The ability to choose between playing one role or another is most likely a function of social background and due also, though to a lesser extent, to the strength of Mars or of aggression in the horoscope. One rather depressing factor is, of course, that thieves go on thieving. For certain socio-economic groups rehabilitation is rarely successful. The rate of recidivism — the proportion of those criminals who return to crime — is very high. Saturn's connection with chronic states, whether physical or emotional, describes this astrologically. Today much of the work being carried out by criminologists is concerned with the psychology of the chronic victim, the view being that every criminal needs his victim and vice versa. In astrology, this makes sense in so far as the same equation can be seen to generate very different modes of behaviour.

Tom Keating, the 'master fake', rocked the art world when he confessed to flooding the market with 'Sexton Blake' paintings. ('Sexton Blake', rhyming slang for 'fake' was Keating's own description of the technique he used to forge the work of such masters as Goya, Tintoretto and Rembrandt.) Something in Keating's character led him to always include in these pictures a trade mark which under X-ray examination would reveal its true origin, for example, a statement like 'This is a fake.' In order to copy these masterpieces he naturally required a very high level of technical proficiency, both in drawing and painting and also at methods of ageing the works. In *The Fake's Progress*[14] he points out that he made no secret of his ability to forge paintings; he boasted of it in pubs and at dinner parties. Keating confessed that doing them was not easy, as it required long, tedious hours of painstaking work, not to mention the amount of time spent scouring junk shops for the right materials. Finding someone to buy the finished product was not that simple, either. Part of the joy in doing the fakes was the amusement he derived from the fact that stuffy dealers were called out to display their alleged expertise. In a sense, this was Mercury's consummate snub to those who thought they knew everything about everything, especially those who purported to know merely by intuition whether a thing was right or not. Once again, the trickster plays upon the vanities of his elders.

Keating's horoscope throws a brilliant perspective on the Mercurial inclination towards imitation. The subject was born at midnight, and his chart typifies a linear structure. Apart from a small triangular pattern composed of Jupiter, Pluto and Neptune, the chart mainly depicts the restless, highly strung disposition of someone whose character is perched on a tightrope of aspects. Keating's Sun-Mars conjunction in Pisces on the IC stands alone. It makes a fitting representative of the dominant creative force, as well as of the individual's capacity to compartmentalize his experience; in addition, it probably indicates the fine tuning abilities he demonstrated when re-creating a Rembrandt or a Goya. Keating admits that in those instances he felt a psychic overshadowing by the artist in question: he felt technically incapable of duplicating works of the great masters without some assistance from them.

Like that of the Great Train Robbery, Keating's map shows a large cluster of planets in the vicinity of the third house and IC area, emphasizing the collusion of friends and family. In fact, Keating's origins were not very different from those of the train robbers. Both charts indicate survival as a partial motivation for their subjects' illustrious tomfoolery. Keating's solution of sending up the culture vultures befits the air-water combination shown in his chart. Mercury's conjunction with Uranus just has to depict the super-shyster — an aspect the two charts have in common. The trines to the Moon here point to Keating's easy manner and success at sales; the Moon's Gemini location near Pluto in the eighth house points to his imitative use of other people's resources. Curiously, in both cases Mars appears in the fourth house, and the MC-IC axis in the two charts is interchangeable; it is almost as if the Mars positions constituted the hidden ingredient necessary for the conversion of ordinary varieties of dishonesty into more aggressive assaults on society. Symbolically, at least, Mars in the fourth embodies the idea of the underdog striving very hard to confront his superiors, who occupy the tenth house.

How, then, can an astrologer detect the signs of criminal activity in the horoscope? Astrology has no way of stating unequivocally x or y pattern equals criminal behaviour. What it can reveal, albeit in a rather crude way, are those traits which suggest an identification with the underdog: namely, low self-esteem, a conscious or unconscious contempt for authority, a high degree of mutability and impulsive, aggressive instincts. The standard problem is: who makes the best crook? Probably the best criminologist! It would seem that social conditioning is more influential than the individual will in the formation of most potential thieves. Uniformly, it is Mercury that gets all of us up to mischief, but whether or not we wind up in gaol is a matter that is far more likely to be determined

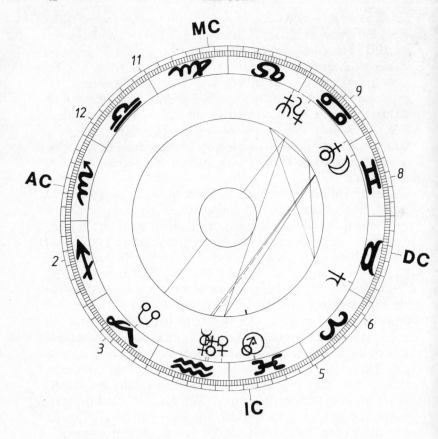

Figure 8   The horoscope chart of Tom Keating.

by socio-economic factors; few upper-class tricksters find themselves detained at Her Majesty's pleasure.

Hermes' confrontation with Zeus illustrates truth-telling with a twist. Zeus, the Greek equivalent of Jupiter, represents formal law, being both judge and juror for mortals and immortals. Hermes' brilliance aroused his sympathies. Though he used his authority to chastise the erring infant, he felt equally compelled to reward his genius. In a similar way, we see the Great Train robbers immortalized in a book and on film for their flagrant breach of social values. And only recently, Tom Keating was in the news again: this time because he had managed to sell paintings that bore *his own* signature. The public never really wanted to be the victim of either stunt; yet deep down most people would probably murmur to themselves that they as individuals would never have been real victims, as they did not possess two and a half million pounds, still less the five hundred needed to buy a phoney El Greco. The key here rests with the unconscious consent that the public give to the flagrant theft of superfluous riches. The motivation is not very different in either direction; each side of the law must contend with its opposite. Astrologically, Mercury and Jupiter form a natural polarity along the axis formed by the third and ninth houses. This opposition is usually defined as that of the higher versus the lower mind. The constant interaction between man's affinity with the primitive, spontaneous nature of lawlessness and his need to civilize those urges within the framework of a higher wisdom accounts for the ambivalence shown when the clever get caught. Man's childish backpedalling into the trickster's role is one that is both familiar and indulged.

Notes

1. Norman O. Brown, *Hermes the Thief: the Evolution of a Myth* (University of Wisconsin Press, 1947). An excellent introduction to the rationale for Mercury's thieving disposition on p.8.
2. Ainsworth, *Introduction to Psychology* (1973) p.83. Harlow's monkey experiments are to be found in any introductory psychology text.
3. *ibid.*
4. *ibid.*, p.83.
5. H. L. Cornell, *Dictionary of Medical Astrology* (Llewellyn Publications, St Paul, Minnesota, 1973). A delightful compendium of what seem like old wives' tales and some very reasonable astro-medical deductions. Contains useful resource material on astrological significators of all kinds.
6. St Augustine, *The Enchiridion*.
7. St Thomas Aquinas.
8. Sissela Bok, *Lying: Moral Choice in Public and Private Life* (Pantheon Books, 1978). Kant quote, p.38. Bok raises a number of useful points concerning duplicity that are not mentioned here.
9. Dante, *The Inferno*.
10. Bok, *Lying,* p.32.
11. Bok, *Lying*. Bok elaborates on the nature of paternalistic lying in one full chapter.

12. Piers Paul Read, *The Train Robbers* (Coronet Books, London, 1978). Details of the robbery taken from this journalistic account.

13. E. J. Hobsbawm, 'Bandits' (1969), epilogue to Read, above.

14. Tom Keating and F. and G. Norman, *The Fake's Progress* (Arrow Books, London, 1978). The swindling success of art faker Tom Keating outlined by fake himself and two sleuthing journalists.

3.
Hermes versus Thoth

The Greeks endowed Mercury with an intellectual brilliance and a savage cunning unbecoming to moral virtue. The last chapter depicted Mercury (Hermes) as a conniving swindler whose central aim was that of outsmarting his rivals. Here, through Egyptian eyes, we get another perspective. As Thoth, Mercury is an officer of the court and the purveyor of divine justice; no longer a villain, he has become the barometer of truth and the agent of good will. [1] While Thoth appears in a variety of animal guises — sometimes a stork, a baboon or jackal, he is usually referred to in the masculine gender. For simplicity, we will continue to refer to Thoth that way. However, from an interpretive standpoint, it is my contention that Thoth introduces the *feminine* valence of the Mercury principle. Unlike Hermes, Thoth relies on internal subjective values rather than external objective ones. The degree to which Mercury relies on either a surface identity or an inner one may be called the Hermes/Thoth continuum. Either variation of Mercury may be expressed constructively or destructively.

Thoth represents truth, substance and the sacred, while Hermes embodies falsehood, form and the profane. Maximum identification with either pole leads one in the opposite direction. (Thus truth at one end of the spectrum might just cheat you at the other end of it.)

The first part of this chapter looks at those distinctions between Hermes and Thoth which render one the outpost of moral turpitude and the other the bedrock of righteousness, while the second part presents those horoscope factors which contribute to a Hermes or Thoth predisposition. The final section considers the charts of two individuals, a medium and a lawyer, who articulate the desire to express the truth. In both instances, Mercury is tested first as a 'vehicle' for that objective and second as a probable or improbable bearer of wisdom.

Throughout the history of astrology, Mercury's prime allegiance has been to the Sun, as their physical proximity confirms. Myth also accords a solar influence, but by virtue of familial relationship. Hermes' kinship with the Sun is through brotherhood, whereas Thoth's tie with it is as its eldest son. While Hermes forms a lateral or sibling relationship with Apollo, Thoth's bond with Ra is vertical, that of a son with his father. Hermes' link with Apollo is based on rivalry; Thoth's interaction with Ra reflects a respect for authority. Hermes appears as punk *provocateur,* but Thoth behaves as the humble servant. Hermes' inclination for flight suggests rulership by Gemini; Thoth's discriminating and honourable nature implies Virgo's influence. Although both the Greeks and the Egyptians dubbed Mercury the messenger god, to the former race, he was little more than a cosmic scapegoat for the irrational impulses of gods and men. Hermes was accountable for his actions to all Olympus, not only to the great Zeus.

Thoth was answerable only to Ra. The Egyptians placed him in positions of high responsibility, first as the scribe of the Sun god and then as the advocate of the dead, from whom he extracted confessions during the famed funerary ceremonies. Whereas Hermes straddled the boundaries of justice, Thoth enforced them. On no occasion do we find Thoth engaged in mischievous plots, nor given undignified titles such as 'prince of thieves'. Hermes' conquest of Zeus by wit has no parallel in Egyptian myth; Thoth may use language to defend Horus, but he does so in the name of justice, not in the cause of self-protection. Thoth upholds Ma'at, the goddess of truth: he is the guardian of conscience and the implementer of wisdom. Mercury in the Greek mould is an aimless, peripatetic soul who feeds on knotty situations: conflict and dithering are his *modus operandi.* Thoth, as the lunar deity, embodies rhythm and mystery. He is the retriever of the eye. (The loss of an eye traditionally occurred during eclipses and new Moon phases.) Thoth represents movement, but that which is timeless and subject to renewal: he is the restorer. Mercury's borderline character disposes him towards divination. His curiosity alone would have been enough to lead him to this field, but so would the opportunity it offered him of getting the better of his father, the mighty King of Olympus.

Hermes coveted Apollo's wares, especially clairvoyance, but Apollo knew of his half-brother's frivolous streak and recommended that he learn pebble-reading first. Significantly, pebble-reading — divination by physical object — was taught by the Fates: Hermes' first task was that of mastering the physical world and of overcoming the influences which bound him inextricably to the wheel of fortune. This art, like astrology, takes time to learn. Hermes abhors effort, still less that required for laying a foundation for later study; patience and commitment are anathema to him. Moreover, he fears disappointment: like most forms of divination, pebble-reading shatters one's illusion that foreknowledge is always possible. The experienced diviner recognizes that the most accurate readings are the logical extension of a living history based on a precise assessment of character and the probability of a certain type of behaviour. Divination of this order calls for more than merely enthusiasm or a suitably receptive spirit; it demands a high level of self-awareness and a constant vigilance lest the personal or Hermetic does not pass for prophecy. Apollo's reply to Hermes' plea for precognition was then to look inwards, via the framework of his own making. Remember that the name Hermes means 'stones' — landmarks along the highway. To learn the art of pebble-reading, Hermes must of necessity stand guard at his own altar-place.

Mercury of the Hermes variety is *the* consumer in the occult supermarket. Rarely, however, does he linger long enough to do more than touch base with the options; most dilettantes still count on Apollo when it comes to coughing up the secrets. While Hermes seeks foreknowledge, Thoth was born with it: prescience is second nature to him, as is responsibility. While Hermes yearns for the trappings of power (the left path), Thoth observes the cautious route (the right path) wherein occult phenomena are judged real but of little intrinsic interest. Hermes lacks identity; he finds himself through sources beyond himself. He is the master imitator and example of that which is *not centred*. He thrives on the periphery of experience; he never enters it fully. By contrast, Thoth maintains clear value systems and has personal autonomy.

The pull of the supernatural, as with any religious yearning, derives from split parental images. The father is an absent yet idealized, domineering character; the mother an ambiguous, equally idealized but ignored creature. The father is the omniscient tyrant whose word is gospel and whose single vanity stems from his admiration of his spiritual produce/progeny. For this reason he is bemused and blinded by the idiosyncrasies his children display. Although Hermes and Thoth both have fathers of unquestionable authority, Hermes has a negative identification with Zeus, while Thoth internalizes all that is virtue in Ra. Hermes maintains a hostile allegiance to his father king; by contrast, Thoth acts as warrior and

judge on his parent's behalf. Note how in both the Hermes and
the Thoth myths, Mother has the bit part in the whole drama —
the walk-on lines. She is the eclipsed woman, living offstage, in
isolation, outside the privileged area occupied by her deified son.
Maia, Hermes' mother spent her earthly existence inside a cave.
Egyptian mythology makes no reference to Thoth's mother at all,
save indirectly in *Pyramid Text 1271*'s obscure rendering of the
name Thoth as 'Thou hast no mother'.[3] For the Mercury-possessed
soul, the mother may be considered as something of an
embarrassment — the consummate poor relation who is shunted
from cubbyhole to cubbyhole, receiving only the vaguest kind of
recognition and tacit acceptance.

The virgin Mary is another example of a 'special' son's mother
being relegated to the mysterious and thus shoved into the
background: the Catholic's idealized virgin is no less real than the
Protestant's indifferent one. One approach raises Mary to the status
of a deity, whilst the other reduces her to merely the level of a brood
mare. Both deny the feminine principle's earthly connection: one
by raising Mary above it, the other by discounting her role
altogether. Effectively, she is made invisible in that she has no
personality. In a sense then, Mercury is 'immaculate conception'
— it represents spiritual ideas stripped of their earthly aspect, thus
incomplete. Hermes' identity problem rests on his inability to
ground the intellect in some workable construct. His occult
sensibility stems not from any balanced attempt to integrate the
universe but rather from a tendency to play with it or escape.

Modern civilization is indebted to Hermes for those intellectual
contributions which distinguish the masculine principle; yet the
backlash has been a costly one. Bereft of feminine values, Hermes
has adopted a guise of doubting Thomas, arch sceptic and cynical
prig. By reshaping the logical through the diabolical, he has split
feminine principles into the Judaeo-Christian's arch enemy: He,
who twists Scripture. The biblical notion of Satan as consummate
liar as well as repository of evil finds an appropriate double in a
one-eyed Hermes. The quest for balanced vision begins with Thoth.

Thoth's search for identity differs radically from that of Hermes
in that he knows something is missing. He responds to the cosmic
cry 'Where is the Moon?' by following it. The sense of something
being ruptured fuels Thoth's need to know: it is Thoth's process
of discovery that re-establishes the light. Thoth thus defines his
bearings by cataloguing matter. He makes lists; he records that
which is. He is a master librarian and a meticulous researcher. His

mark is a blind eye or one which is somehow injured. The physical condition usually accompanies a fairly pronounced 'blind spot' in the psyche which is both problem and resolution for the Thoth-ruled personality. The damaged eye is the 'evil eye' and symbolizes man's darker aspect; Thoth's regular encounter with darkness assures the shadow its territory, along with the possibility of its expulsion. Unlike Hermes, whose twin-eyed glee keeps him oblivious of the unconscious, Thoth knows all too well the frightful regularity with which darkness falls. His ability to recognize the impediment and do something about it gives him an advantage.

Astrologically, Thoth-ruled Mercury is subject to radical upheavals in terms of action and perspective: violent overhauls can occur overnight, or alternatively, over protracted periods. The thrust of the 'eye' is pain-induced change, and for the Thoth-influenced psyche this is both inevitable and perpetual. Thoth's reality is that of promise, whereby an absence of the Sun or Moon during conditions of an eclipse signals either the beginning or a high point of the life cycle. The privilege of Thoth is that of rhythm of knowing. By contrast, Hermes thrives on movement, however aimless or idle; to this fleet-footed messenger, the question of whether life is or is not out of sync is irrelevant.

How do we know which aspect Mercury uses? What characteristics in a horoscope favour a 'Hermes' interpretation rather than a 'Thoth' one? Knowledge presented to Thoth exists in the form of an awareness of the divine aspects of himself. Hermes, on the other hand, comprises acts of fate. Where Hermes chases shadows, Thoth stands still. Doubt-prone Hermes challenges everything that inhabits his psyche sphere and demands proof of worldly powers. Despite having access to the supernatural force, he is unable to make use of it; he courts danger before his prime, inviting tête-à-têtes with the demonic or taking a crash course in psychedelia. Whatever the nature of the encounter, be it mephistophelean or simply 'day tripping', Hermes' importuning lands him in serious trouble. The modern equivalent occurs when teenagers experiment with mind-altering substances. The naïve, undeveloped personality is excited by psychic stimuli but ill-equipped to process them. Because the person's identity is not yet fully established, this type of psychic flooding can prove quite alarming. Another manifestation of Mercury's is the ouija board. Planchettes may seem to be innocuous playthings, but the fact is that such 'toys' are extremely dangerous instruments when placed in the hands of the suggestible. (This is not the place to discuss the existence of evil as an objective entity. Possession — by whatever source, whether through actual contact with a demon or by one's own consuming negativity — is a disorganizing experience and not one that is recommended for amusement.)

Thoth is a debunker of power; he is no hostage to its allure. Like Christ, he respects authority, but is neither intoxicated nor intimidated by its appearance; he comes to fulfil the law, not to break it. Moreover, he is not likely to be snared by the poison of self-doubt: he moves from an assumption of faith in the truth. Thoth's wisdom puts one in mind of Jesus, who, having fasted for forty days, refused point-blank the devil's challenge to turn stones into bread. When asked by his Master to walk on the water, Peter found his faith faltering at the intrusion of Hermes' wind; thus afraid, he began to sink. Jesus' comment was: 'How little faith you have! Why did you doubt?'

Table 2   Horoscope Factors: Hermes vs Thoth

Hermes type: kinetic / masculine / form

Communication, whether true or false, seems banal in content, ostensibly objective and usually of transient significance. Subject to tricks, mishaps, distortion of surface truths.

(a) Weak aspect structure. Boundaries between self and environment unreliable. Poor controls on will.

(b) Weak Sun and Saturn. Ego vulnerable to flattery, false reality. Low self-esteem. Responsibility development slow.

(c) Aspect alignment lateral / horizontal. Motivation for contact, personal involvement. Linear maps, when horizontal by direction, are very Hermetic.

(d) Mercury-Uranus tie. Erratic, nervous disposition. Exaggerates Hermes' nature because it is usually operating unconsciously.

(e) Gemini emphasis. Precocious experimentation. Low discrimination. Versatility. Corresponds to youth / adolescence phase.

(f) Mercury cusp or pre-cusp. Environmental demands placed on Hermes. Extreme agitation, movement.

(g) Maximum elongation from the Sun. Mercury has freedom to act when far from the Sun.

Thoth type: static / feminine / substance

Communication, whether true or false, seems profound in content, transpersonal in nature and timeless. Subject to moralizing, strict value judgements.

(a) Aspect structure coherent. Grounded by strong aspects patterns and balance of aspect type.

(b) Strong ego planets: Sun, Moon and Saturn all healthy, congruent.

(c) Aspect alignment vertical. Aspiration for individuation, higher knowledge.

(d) Mercury ties to Saturn and Pluto. Substance, depth. Pluto overstates Thoth's role when it is functioning unconsciously.

(e) Virgo emphasis. Discrimination. Experiences in maturity.

(f) Mercury on low point. Frustrated communication. Withdrawal from words. Emphasis on inner development because one is never heard or understood.

(g) Mercury Cazimi. Precise expression of solar wishes. God = Messenger = One.

(h) Neutral planets (Moon, Jupiter, Neptune) enhance Mercury's receptivity. They carry no gender of their own. How these are used by an individual is contingent on the general slant of a horoscope, whether toward Hermes or Thoth.

The Horoscope Features of Hermes / Thoth Orientation

The most important factor in determining either a Hermes or Thoth orientation is the horoscope's aspect structure. Solid, well-knit charts suggest strength of character strength as well as adherence to principle: such maps infer the protection of Thoth. Incomplete aspect structures signal a low stress threshold and a malleable nature that is somewhat typical of Hermes. The second consideration relevant to a perspective of Mercury is the aspect alignment: do the aspects form vertical or lateral movements? *Lateral aspects* suit the Hermes rubric because they multiply options and accept the world at face value. Hermes observes the world through a wide-angle lens: the horizon becomes broadened and flattened. Everything is taken in; nothing is differentiated. Contact is the lateral chart's main theme. For Hermes, this usually implies *indiscriminate* liaisons with the environment. Because relationship for relationship's sake is a high Hermes priority, here Mercury slips into a lot of game-playing. Such manipulations are aimed not at the preservation of one relationship in particular but rather at maintaining the desired condition of contact with anyone.

A preoccupation with relationship necessarily short-circuits the individuation process: the failure to acquire personal autonomy generally results not only in disappointment where relationships are concerned but also in some form of alienation. Dissatisfaction leads Hermes to another kind of interaction, namely therapy. It is within this context that the Hermes' trickster motif unravels itself. Wiggling out of a tight squeeze is Hermes' forte and one that is perfected in the climate afforded by therapy. Typical would be the Hermes habit of changing the subject mainstream at the moment of confrontation; another would be the Freudian slip, the inadvertent use of the wrong word or reference which betrays the speaker's bias. The 'talking cure' has its limitations: the same thing that evinces growth (communication) contributes to the impasse (talking and not doing). 'Be here now' people insist that living in the encounter zone (the horizon axis) is the way to solve problems, but for the laterally motivated person that may be the very last thing that is required.

Vertical Charts
Thoth rules the *vertical* mentality. The world is stratified along socio-economic, moral and intellectual lines. Hierarchical thinking narrows the focus so that the world is viewed through a telephoto lens. Thoth's view is both distant and selective; too much of it in a chart introduces patronizing, occasionally snooty behaviour — airs. Mercury suffers not so much from overexposure (Hermes' plight) as from inhabiting a rarefied atmosphere. Depth of perspective can manifest as tunnel vision. If vertical charts sound dictatorial, then lateral charts risk doormat status. The need for balance demands that the authoritarian should incorporate a bit of the egalitarian and vice versa: those with vertical charts might stoop a bit to conquer, while 'flat earth' types are advised to sample the ozone beyond their immediate periphery.

Mercury Aspects
Mercury's aspects further define the Hermes/Thoth effect. The feminine planets (Venus, Saturn and Uranus) belong to Thoth; the masculine ones (Mars, the Sun and Pluto) to Hermes. The Sun operates through Hermes, except when it forms a precise conjunction, an exception that will be explained later.

Ego Structure

The ego planets the Sun, Moon and Saturn form Mercury's reference point. If the Sun and Saturn are weak (independent of any aspect to Mercury) this means diminished will-power and impulse control; confidence is weak, as is discrimination. Hermes responds to this condition by exhibiting an exaggerated diffusion and uncertainty. If the Sun and Saturn are powerful, they discipline Mercury, a cue to which Thoth responds.

Gender

The Moon, like Mercury, is neuter; it reiterates any themes that Mercury activates. Planetary gender is obvious in the cases of Venus and Mars. Mercury aspects to Venus ensure that Thoth's clear ethical and aesthetic sense will prevail: here Mercury moves from the position of values in the world. Mercury-Mars ties bestow Hermes' quick, sharp intellect. The Venus-Thoth association establishes beauty and stability, while the Mars-Hermes link guarantees movement and change — characteristics that are considered essentially masculine.

Less apparent to the astrologer are Uranus' essential femininity and Pluto's basic masculinity. Unless the influence of these planets is rendered fully conscious, the personality overcompensates by showing the opposite effect: Mercury-Uranus thus reads as a negative Hermes and Mercury-Pluto as a negative Thoth. Uranus threatened by its own genuine femininity comes on as the ultra-macho anarchist. If overcompensated, Uranus *denies* the feminine impulse for structure by destroying security systems and inventing new ones; in so doing it appears cold, heartless and alien. It represses all signs of dependency, simulating strength in order to cut the apron strings. One structure is abolished in favour of another, more sophisticated one that is often more hide-bound than its predecessor. This planet may seem radical, but lift the lid on it and you will reveal a hierarchy of fear related specifically to the issue of safety and protection. Uranus's disruptive, chaotic quality stems from an inherent rigidity which makes it psychologically brittle.

Pluto resists the masculine elements of its make-up. In particular, it avoids the direct confrontation or overt exercise of power associated with either Sun or Mars. Pluto's silent indirect approach is both seductive and subversive. It wins by intimidation. Pluto undeveloped denies its need to exercise the will: it conceals its drive for independence and volition. A rejection of Pluto constitutes a denial that one seeks omniscience. Feminine withdrawal is one way that Pluto eclipses its own aggressive spirit; behind the facade of helplessness and false modesty reign ambition and its ally, rivalry. Mercury in relationship to either of these outer planets gives an individual insight into both its Hermes and its Thoth sides. As a rule, however, the shadow effect dominates, so that Mercury-Uranus turns up as Hermes' master trickster and Mercury-Pluto looms forth as Thoth's diabolic counterpart, the magician.

Sign Emphasis

The sign of Gemini amplifies a Hermes affinity, as does the condition of comparative youth, children being far more likely than 'civilized' adults to adopt the wayward Mercurial style of behaviour. Virgo aligns with Thoth's make-up: the Virgoan discrimination where values are concerned means that it accords exceptionally strongly with Thoth virtue.

Cusp and Pre-cusp Positions

Mercury positioned on the cusp or pre-cusp is quintessentially Hermes. These souls usually look the part as well: their movement, gestures and speed of communication all typify Mercury's Greek outfit. Cuspal Mercury has an anxious, restless quality which is invariably exhausting to the environment; such persons are full of tricks and given to the irritating habit of never shutting up. Just as these individuals tire their surroundings, so too do they tire themselves, giving way to mental fatigue. Pre-cuspal Mercury is especially prone to nervous tension. Such placements give individuals a breathless quality, they seem never to slow down and to be permanently desperate about something or other.

Cazimi

Mercury on Cazimi (within seventeen minutes of arc from the Sun) describes the perfect alliance between God and his messenger, Ra and Thoth: here congruence between thought and action reaches its peak. Truth in the objective sense may or may not register, but what does come forth is truth in its purest subjective expression. In order to assess the quality of the truth that is outpoured a separate examination of the individual's purpose is necessary. Cazimi planets have always baffled astrologers. Some maintain that such positions strengthen the planet as much as combustion debilitates it, while others, like J. Wilson, postulate that a Cazimi planet 'is undoubtedly in the worst state of combustion'[4] — presumably burnt to a cinder! My own view is that Cazimi status accentuates Mercury's role. The degree of reliability is nevertheless coloured by the overall structure of the horoscope in question.

Combust

Mercury Combust (within five degrees of the Sun) is something altogether different. Here subjectivity, though still prominent, masquerades as objectivity. A thread of self-righteousness often runs through subjects with combust Mercury: such persons believe they are conscious of their own blind spots and faults. Their concentration, though keen, tends to appear one-sided and their views are somewhat parochial.

Low Point

Mercury on a low point may be equally compulsive in its need to communicate; the results, however, are far less rewarding. Here Mercury suffers from frustration when it comes to articulating ideas. Such persons are constantly being misinterpreted or, worst of all, totally ignored. Mercury on a low point will often interrupt discussions with seemingly irrelevant, off-the-wall remarks. A close examination shows that these are often comments on a topic long ago dropped from the conversation. The time-lag necessary for low point Mercury to organize his or her thoughts is such that by the time he or she does blurt out a few tentative phrases these are met with dead silence. Unlike pre-cuspal or cuspal Mercury, which simply barges right into the discussion, Mercury low point waits and waits. Part of Mercury's difficulty when on a low point lies in the fact that it despises strait-jackets. Low points, being the most 'fixed' area within a house, are not the Mercurial ideal: their atmosphere is claustrophobic. The resolution of a low point Mercury comes easiest through meditation: the pursuit of inner guidance rather than external feedback softens the blow that was suffered. A low point Mercury must withdraw from any overt attempt to influence or command attention verbally. Communication works best when made in such a way that others or the environment approach the subject first rather than the other way round. Silence is low point Mercury's best strategy.

Elongation from the Sun

Mercury's elongation from the Sun adds another dimension to the Hermes/Thoth continuum. The German astrologer Busse[5] divided Mercury's maximum distance from the Sun (28°) into three sectors. In his opinion, Mercury nearest to the Sun indicated those who were motivated by highly subjective values: in other words, the dictator type. He allotted the area covered by the second ten degrees to the academic realm; there Mercury was said to be dry, intellectual and comparatively detached. He equated Mercury at the maximum elongation with an artistic sense; but personally, I find Mercury at greatest distance far more imaginative and experimental. While Thoth clearly prefers to keep close to the Sun for guidance, Hermes enjoys the greater freedom afforded him when occupying the outer limits of the Sun.

Mercury and Mediumship

Investigations into the lives and horoscopes of practising mediums have shown that no single astrological factor denotes psychic ability. Problems arise when it comes to research because of the multiplicity of forms that mediumship can take, the varying degree of skill involved and the reliability of the performer, not to mention the additional factor of personal bias. Especially problematic for the clinical observer is the fact that spiritualist mediums (those included in the sample were predominantly spiritualists) rarely place symbols and/or impressions within a specific context; information is transmitted in bits and pieces, the sitter being obliged to complete the equation. The communication is thus hit-and-miss: this may be due to factors unconnected with the mediumship. For example, short- and long-term memory were notably absent among my sample: most were unable either to give detailed chronological histories of their lives as mediums or to pinpoint circumstances of importance in their early years. Another common feature amongst the mediums of my sample was that their formal education had been either irregular or in some way curtailed; the opportunity to develop the appropriate screening and interpretive skills had in most instances simply not been available.

Exhaustive statistical work on this sample was performed by A. T. Oram.[6] The results so far are inconclusive. Meanwhile, the working hypothesis is that Mercury should be active in the realm of psychic phenomena, the reasoning — albeit circular and a classical astrological pitfall — being as follows: Mercury rules communication; therefore it should be present in psychic communiqués. We know that Mercury is a conundrum: that it plays tricks, but that sometimes it does not. From this standpoint it is irrelevant whether mediumistic events are *genuine* messages from higher beings, tricks played on us by the unconscious or the results of sleight of hand, for Mercury rules all three categories. Fraudulent mediumship has long been an important issue among psychical researchers. The fact that 'good' subjects have later demonstrated elements of deception is not particularly helpful. Personally, I am not convinced that the existence of isolated cases of fraud justifies the view that all mediumship is suspect.

The fundamental characteristic of mediumship is neutrality: the sensitive's apparatus is a film upon which impressions of either sound or symbol are etched. Such impressions may or may not be intelligible. A medium supposedly gets information that is free of prejudice. The question is: is this really possible? Can one expect an individual's 'film' to be entirely free of its own imprint? Good mediums are capable of receiving subtle signals and are also skilled at making sense of them. Spiritualist mediums often describe themselves as 'telephones', an analogy that would seem apt when they are functioning at optimum level; unfortunately, however, such mediums rarely sustain a high degree of receptivity. The personality invariably intrudes into what is ostensibly understood as direct communication from discarnate bodies; fuzzy messages may thus simply be a kind of spirit 'crossed line'. Artists and musicians make the best mediums, as they are blessed with an exquisite sensitivity plus a superior means of expression, yet they are no less subject to impasses or blocks in their creative flow — ego constrictions jam the mechanism. Neutrality, characteristic of Mercury, is also found in the Moon, Jupiter and Neptune. The presence of a strong Mercury alone is insufficient for signs of 'receptivity': one must seek evidence of flexibility or openness from all four neutral agents. In addition, one must always return to the aspect structure for clues regarding motivation, purpose and unusual ability. Because ego factors probably play an important role in the apparent 'failure' of mediumistic function, one must also make note of the precise relationship that exists between the Sun, the Moon and Saturn. Mercury's ongoing task is that of translating what is initially gibberish into some meaningful context and rechannelling it back into the environment. A consistently high-level intelligence, whatever its origin, is hardly likely to be filtered through ordinary channels, nor are trivialities likely to be transmitted through superior ones. Therefore the astrologer should first examine the composition of the aspect structure for signs of unique talent and then check Mercury for any indicators of the ability to express it. However, astrology is certainly not the final arbiter when it comes to judging the authenticity of a medium's source.

The Horoscope of a Medium

Elizabeth Farrell is a well-known spiritualist medium currently teaching at the College of Psychic Studies in London. Her

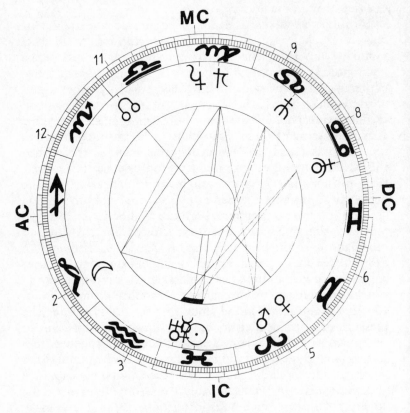

Figure 9   The horoscope chart of Elizabeth Farrell.

mediumship began in 1964, when she uncovered various gifts: clairaudience, clairvoyance, psychometry and a capacity for trance. In 1980, on the advice of her spirit guide, 'Nemerah', she gave up the trance work which she had been carrying out for nine years in favour of 'spontaneous inspiration' lectures. According to Mrs Farrell herself, trance mediumship and inspirational lecturing differ from each other in that the first uses the guide's thought and speech patterns while the second draws on the guide's thought but is produced through the medium's own speech pattern. Her favourite method of spirit communication is clairaudience.

The first task in judging a map is to examine motivation: what governs the individual's life force, what makes him or her tick? Motivation is determined by the direction and structure of the aspects. The overall structure of Mrs Farrell's is three-pronged, suggesting a minimal interest in security or the status quo. Her life is not, despite the Moon's second cusp placement here, overly concerned with acquisition. Had Mrs Farrell's chart shown a four-sided aspect structure, this would have been quite the reverse: her world would have been dictated by a need to sustain familiar patterns. The aspects rise from the base of the chart up to the midheaven and ninth house. The presence of several oppositions from three to nine indicate a life commitment to the realm of ideas. Teaching and the pursuit of knowledge constitute the main working objective. The planets' upward thrust is supported by a 'dominant learning' triangle (Moon-Jupiter-Mars) and a 'seeker' pattern (Sun-Neptune-Mars). The first pattern, dominant learning, anchors the medium. It emphasizes a gutlike intuition: Mrs Farrell simply knows things at a subliminal level. The Moon and Jupiter stretch her awareness, while Mars strengthens her instinct. The second trio, denoting the seeker, adds a spiritual note. A longing for truth is one facet of the Piscean influences which fuse intelligence with compassion. Here Mercury is both angel and healer, its expression gentle and soothing yet charged with Uranian insight. Mercury, strong by degree, and number of vertical aspects guarantees that communication will play a substantial role in this person's life. Although found here in the position of its ostensible fall or detriment, Mercury is nevertheless empowered by its degree position. Planets on or near 11°32′ of a sign display the best aspects of that sign's character; thus Mercury in Pisces would give maximum sensitivity minus the muddle.

The ancients claimed that Mercury in the third house was 'accidentally dignified' because it inhabited native soil. The Hubers have found that a planet falling in its favourite house (i.e. Mercury in the third or sixth house) may nevertheless experience a frustration of planetary energy when occupying a low point. Here, the subject's Mercury-Jupiter opposition tenants that space. Low point planets focus energy inwardly: they incubate. Moreover, a low point means a resistance to formal instruction: such subjects learn by experience instead; their energies blossom late. As a matter of fact, Elizabeth Farrell's mediumship began comparatively recently, at a time when transiting Saturn, Uranus and Pluto moved back and forth over a sensitive Virgo-Pisces axis. Because Mrs Farrell's Mercury in Pisces (10°50′) shows her acute sensitivity, and its low point location suggests a struggle for effective communication, I suspect that the early school years proved very difficult for her, *not* because of a lack of intelligence or ability but rather because effective communication operates on a two-way basis: in order to be useful, words must be heard and understood. Her teachers were probably unable to make sense of that timid brilliance, and the feedback they provided was probably either negligible or unhelpful. As a result, Mercury was obliged to gather resources from another domain. These strengths accumulated over time and were finally recognized in the subject's early forties.

To recap, then, we find Elizabeth Farrell motivated by knowledge and relatively unconcerned with material well-being. (That is not to say that she doesn't manage rather nicely, with the Moon's trine to Saturn-Jupiter!) The ego appears stable, and her receptivity is quite high, due to extreme mutability by house/sign, a cuspal Moon and the quincunx-trine-semi-sextile configurations. The drive for higher knowledge is reaffirmed by the inclusion of Sun-Mars-Neptune in the figure. One also senses here a disposition that is world-weary, somewhat vexed by human foibles. Both aspect combinations, dominant and seeker, are fuelled by a third, unpredictable one which I call the 'electric cattle prod'; irritation (Sun-Mars-Jupiter) jolts the system just at those moments of maximum complacency. These patterns, more than any other, are subject to erratic, unconscious handling. Uncontrolled irritation aspects (opposition-quincunx-semi-sextile) work like ill-used scalpels, cutting out the healthy in search of the disease: mental and emotional efficiency suffers as a result. Irritation triangles can lead to tetchiness, especially when exacerbated by edgy planets like Mercury, Mars and Uranus: persons with such structures are decidedly jumpy. The deliberate use of the 'scalpel's tip', the point at which the opposition meets the quincunx, softens the quality of peevishness. Elizabeth Farrell uses her scalpel's tip (Jupiter in Virgo in the ninth) in her regular activities of teaching and clairvoyance.

The ego is a reasonably balanced one: the Moon throws a trine to Saturn, and the Sun makes indirect contact with both the Moon and Saturn via an opposition to Jupiter. All three ego planets, Sun, Moon and Saturn, display power by sign, house or aspect. However, the Sun, due to its strong degree and number of aspects, has a slight edge over the other two: her mediumship will thus function under solar guidance and Mercury's primary bias will be mental. Her Sun-Mercury conjunction depicts a happy alignment between God and the servant. Mercury in the same sign as the Sun concentrates expression, synchronizing thought with action. Close to the Sun, Mercury also maximizes the individual's subjectivity and his or her sense of the union between the ego's demand and its messenger's compliance. Mercury aspects all three outer planets, suggesting access to all forms of higher intelligence: physical, emotional and mental. Furthermore, Mercury rules the midheaven, signifying one's conscious aim, and forms tight oppositions and a mutual reception to the ruler of the ascendant, Jupiter.

Returning to our Hermes-Thoth rating, how does Elizabeth Farrell rank? Is she more likely to fall victim to the pranks of Mercury's Hermes side or to heed the sage Thoth?

HERMES	THOTH
Gemini emphasis by third house	Strong Sun-Moon-Saturn
	Virgo emphasis (by sign)
Mercury-Uranus tie	Mercury-Pluto aspect
Neptune slips back and forth either way	Vertical structure
	Mercury low point
Total number of points: 2	Total number of points: 5

Table 3   Hermes vs. Thoth influences in the chart of Elizabeth Farrell.

Allowing one point for each factor, it would seem that Elizabeth Farrell rests well within the Thoth category.

One Tough Cowboy

Wyoming attorney Gerry Spence is one tough cowboy; he is also a survivor. He says: 'When I walk into a courtroom I am only another hunter, in that dark arena where men are the game and the hunter is also hunted. I stalk the witness on the witness stand, struggle with my adversary, and at some critical moment it becomes a fight to the death.'[7] A trial lawyer's hero, Spence wins because he both listens and does his homework. He is not, as he puts it 'one of the gentlemen in grey' who bankroll millions as counsels to multinational corporations; he abhors legal pundits who would perpetuate pseudo-justice in the name of the mighty dollar. Spence champions the little people: those souls who have either been trampled on by immense corporations or tormented by a twist of fate and whose very lives may depend on his passion for justice.

What evidence does his horoscope show of this winning combination? How is it that here Mercury manages to juggle both hats, Hermes and Thoth, and come out tops?

The striking feature of this chart is its spiky appearance. Aspects

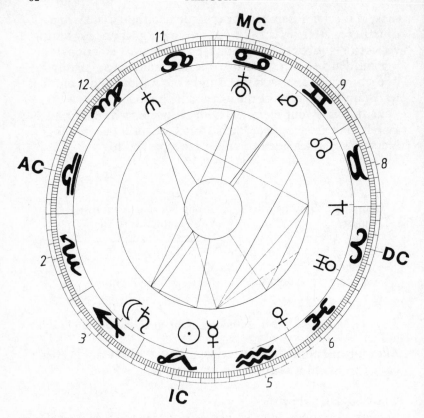

Figure 10 The horoscope chart of Gerry Spence.

jut out in all directions, giving Spence a rather formidable exterior
and a definite resistance to being pigeon-holed. The elevated Mars
and Pluto add to the somewhat ornery, cocksure image that he
projects. Planets lean to the west, revealing his heavy reliance on
other people. This is confirmed by the Libra ascendant — litigation
does, after all, require an open enemy! Locomotive in shape, this
map discloses an unbelievably strong physical drive and stamina.
The planets galvanize around three oppositions: Sun-Pluto, Moon-
Saturn-Mars and Venus-Neptune. Energy is high, as is ambition;
the aspects climb appreciably, assuring that Spence will rise above
his station at birth.

Personalities with vertical charts are especially sensitive to rank and position in the community: they are status-seekers, but only within the hierarchy of their chosen fields. A baker, for example, would not be satisfied to merely make the best bread; he would want to be *known* for making the best bread and perhaps for selling it to the best people. (A baker's wife with the same chart direction might have quite different criteria for status!) The midheaven sign, aspects and planets all give clues as to the kind of status that is sought. Vertical temperaments are often classified as overachievers. It is not that they possess greater ability than others; it is simply that they focus it earlier and with greater force. Horizontal maps have just as strong a chance of success or failure, the difference being that this type of individual cares more,.thus investing more energy in the pursuit of success. Definition of self rests on scaling some ladder of achievement. The horizontal personality's success vector is relationship-oriented, less emphasis being placed on outer or worldly accomplishment. For the vertical type, frustration of status is intolerable. This frustration is frequently dealt with in one of two ways: the watery, introspective type ascribes failure to personal ineptitude and inherent blundering, whereas the more fiery, outgoing type blames the world, 'them'. Both defences conceal resentment and self-pity, the classic causes of a chip on the shoulder.

Gerry Spence is clearly an overachiever. He wanted to be a hot-shot lawyer from an early age. He worked extremely hard at law school, finishing first in his class; from the hierarchical standpoint, being first, on top, is central to one's identity. Two main themes govern Spence's chart: a dominant learning triangle (Mercury-Jupiter-Neptune) and an irritation pattern (Sun-Moon-Pluto). The first structure brings unusual perception. Sensitivity is one of Spence's most reliable tools, as is his understanding of voice nuance and intonation. Dominant learning patterns are one's most essential support systems: they colour everything one does. Spence's version, made up of three neutral planets, makes him a human weathervane; his mind is alert and vigilant, ever ready for a shift in the wind.

Spence's jungle is the courtroom: Mercury-Jupiter squares were born there. A master of rhetoric and of pedagogical tricks, Mercury-Jupiter finds itself equally at home at church or in school. One might think that Jupiter's expansive side would make Mercury-Jupiter bombastic, rather full of itself — but not necessarily. The Mercury-Jupiter square *can* be the model of understatement. What does trickle through, however, is a lesson or moral question, with some spoken or unspoken assumption about how things *should* be. Mercury-Jupiter sharpens the intellect along with the sense of irony:

the Mind moves logically and philosophically, seeking laws in nature. The link with Neptune broadens mental interests as well as sympathies. Spence's Mercury and Jupiter are unusually significant because they form partile parallels to each other (22S10) and a tight parallel to the Sun (22S18). Astrologers tend to overlook parallels of declination. This is definitely a mistake, for parallels seem every bit as potent as the conjunction-opposition team: planets in aspect by longitude and by parallel are extremely powerful. Cases such as Spence's, in which the planets make parallel aspects but no major ties by longitude, are especially intriguing. The subject's legal brilliance is further substantiated by the Sun-Mercury-Jupiter parallels.

Mercury quincunx Neptune upstages any debater: the quincunx, is inimical to even the best of relationships, and resists balance. It causes ideas, whether relevant or not, to drop out of thin air. The quincunx's ruse is that of surprise: anyone with a Mercury quincunx can jar even the staidest or most implacable of assailants. The ruse can also backfire on oneself. A deliberate use of this pesky aspect tames its skittish ways. Considering that quincunxes rule the houses (sixth to eighth) flanking that of one's open foes (seventh), it makes sense that these aspects should be able to operate from the left field. Spence's genius shows itself in his ability to make oblique statements with a straight face: Mercury-Neptune sweetens the tongue along with the sidewinding, so that the jury never knew what hit them. Exhibit A is a classic quip made by Spence: sidling up to an old West jury, to whom spurs and a stetson are Sunday best, Spence asked them point-blank: 'Would you believe a man in a brown velvet suit?'

Sun-Moon-Pluto mobilizes Spence's passion. What better mixture is there for someone who identifies with the underdog yet is able to topple corporate superpowers? Those relentless nags, irritation forms, goad one to achieve particular accomplishments. The specifics of the task are symbolized by that planet which receives both the opposition and the quincunx — in this case, Pluto. Pluto on the scalpel's tip, especially on the Midheaven, mandates a power struggle. Spence must wage war against the ill-considered or unreasonable use of power. Not only must he reform those drives within himself, but he must also impose that challenge on outside authority. Pluto-related themes feature in most of his cases such as those involving murder and negligence. Spence's biggest victory, Silkwood v. Kerr-McGee, a negligence case involving ten and a half million dollar actually involved Plutonium contamination that was responsible for the deaths of factory employees. The famous case has been recently retold in the film *Silkwood.*

However ebullient he may appear, the presence of the Sun, the Moon and Saturn near the IC anchors the perspective inwardly. The ego planets are all strong, by aspect as well as by house position. The Sun retains a slight advantage because of its fourth cusp angularity, enabling Mercury, though predominantly mental, to slip back and forth between intellectual, emotional and practical values; this explains why Spence is a first-rate communicator able to relate to people on any level. Third house planets reveal one's role in the 'small groups' process. The ego triad placed there accounts for his firm commitment to the training of lawyers in effective communication. (He was the first to implement role-playing techniques for helping lawyers in trial practice.) He declares: 'Trial law is not trickery. It is not just technique but much more — it is *understanding* what is happening to human beings in that silent place, the courtroom. To win one must also *care.'*[8] To paraphrase: 'Trial law is not Mercury. It is not just Mercury but much more.' Trickery and technique *do* count for something. Hermes must show his clever tongue and lightning-speed reaction time in order to keep on top of the opposition in a courtroom duel. Winning needs an extra oomph — conviction first, endurance second.

How, then, does Gerry Spence fare on the Hermes/Thoth schema? What sign is there that Mercury functions for the highest purpose?

HERMES	THOTH
Gemini emphasis (Mars, third house)	Strong Sun and Saturn, Moon
	Strong aspect structure
Mercury-Uranus tie	Vertical aspect structure

Table 4   Hermes vs. Thoth factors in the chart of Gerry Spence.

The Mercury tie to Neptune and Jupiter form a part of a dominant learning pattern: therefore the weight is carried to Thoth.

Notes

1. Patrick Boylan, *Thoth, Hermes of Egypt: A Study of Some Aspects of Theological Thought in Ancient Egypt* (Oxford University Press, 1922). The best source material on Thoth. An especially useful section in his appendix material which includes 'Epithets of Thoth' taken from Egyptian papyri.
2. J. Viau, *Egyptian Mythology* (Hamlyn, London) Background material to the Thoth myth.
3. Pyramid Text 1271. (Found in Appendix to Boylan.)
4. J. Wilson, *Complete Dictionary of Astrology* (Samuel Weiser, New York, 1970). An excellent work of reference for explanations of astrological terminology.
5. Busse work.
6. Arthur T. Oram, 'Mercury-Mars-Pluto in the Charts of Mediums' in *Astrological Journal*, 1983. A statistical evaluation of the horoscopes of professional mediums in the UK.
7. Gerry Spence and Anthony Polk, *Gunning for Justice: My Life and Trials* (Doubleday, 1982). Spence's biographical material extracted for this autobiography and from a television interview (*Sixty Minutes* programme).
8. Spence and Polk, *Gunning for Justice*, p.326.

4.

Thoroughly Modern Mercury

To be, or not to be — that is the question.
> William Shakespeare, *Hamlet*

To be, or not to be — that is the answer.
> *Mercury*

Long before Uranus jumped on the astrological bandwagon, Mercury introduced themes that were altogether modern, namely conflict and alienation. Hamlet's struggle hinges on the fact that he poses the issues of 'being' and 'not-being' in terms of a question. Here the conflict arises from moral/ethical values and one's sense of obligation to choose one course of action as opposed to another. Hamlet invites self-doubt and war by assuming that one choice is more valuable than another. The thrust of existentialism, the core philosophy of the twentieth century, is that life is a series of options and the individual is 'condemned' to choose; not choosing is in itself a form of choice. Mercury's rejoinder implies that options exist and that choice is probable, however incidental or irrelevant it may be. Unfettered Mercury operates beyond an ethical framework such as that prescribed by Kant's 'categorical imperative'; it favours a situational ethic whereby decisions are made from circumstance. The irony here is that no matter how indifferent Mercury may be to the realm of values, its very indifference constitutes a kind of existential choice. Its marriage to the modern rests on its view of 'being' as provisional and value-free.

Choice implies duality: it is impossible to choose unless one simultaneously confronts an 'either/or' in some form or other. Western logic was born with Aristotle's basic definition of logic as a choice between A and not-A: logically, something cannot be both A and not-A at one and the same time. Nevertheless, until a century ago clear lines of guidance existed as to whether one should choose A or not-A: God was in his heaven, and heaven was where one wanted to go. To be good was to get there while to be bad was not to. In modern times the lines have become blurred; little is offered in the way of clarification on the subject of what is good and what is bad. We have to evaluate — to choose — constantly. Duality in thinking (and with it the options in choosing) has extended its influence since the days of Aristotle; it formed the cornerstone of the work of the first 'modern' philosopher, René Descartes. Descartes understood duality in terms of a mind/body split, but he did so within a historical context where all thinking was becoming dualistic. [1] With the rise of capitalism, Aristotle's original 'either/or' got totally out of hand. All of a sudden we lived in a consumer world where we could choose between one breakfast cereal and another — the instruments with which we choose being our minds, not our bodies. Mercury is the 'choice' *par excellence,* the planet without meaning in itself who has to get meaning from somewhere else; thus it has to choose. It is also the planet without a 'body'. Mercury, as I shall explain later, is without sensuality: it is the 'mind' side of the dualistic split implied in Cartesian thought, understood at its core as the divorce from the body. Although I cannot explore all these issues here, they will be illustrated further if I spend a little time with the first of the moderns, Descartes, then with Nietzsche, who understood the trap that duality and choice set up, and finally with Andy Warhol, who fell into it.

René Descartes. March 31, 1596, Le Haye, France, 2.00 a.m. LMT (disputed data)

Sun 10 Aries 32	Moon 5 Taurus 13
Mercury 29 Aries 28	Venus 5 Taurus 46
Mars 22 Gemini 01	Jupiter 15 Aries 18
Saturn 2 Virgo 12 retrograde	Uranus 15 Aries 37
Neptune 16 Leo 02 retrograde	Pluto 17 Aries 41
Ascendant 10 Capricorn 32	Midheaven 11 Scorpio 03

Table 5 Horoscope data for René Descartes (Lois Rodden, *The American Book of Charts).*

Descartes's topheavy fire-earth chart ensures that here Mercury will perceive a *literal* separation between mind and body. The mental divorced from the physical, ungrounded and without anchor, creates a fertile territory for alienation. Fire and earth represent opposites, and when both these elements are very strong in a chart, there will be a tendency for the individual to establish clear distinctions between one form of reality and another. Astrologers generally assign fire to the concept of intuition and earth to the category of sensation. Intuition is connected with the mind and thinking (although this is not identical to air's thinking quality), and sensation fits very neatly into the body symbolism. Thus one sees already the ingredients necessary in Descartes's horoscope for his particular interest in the age-old problem of duality. Central to the Cartesian approach is the idea that 'thinking' equals 'being', as embodied in the familiar phrase *'Cogito, ergo sum'*, translated as 'I think, therefore I am.' While Mercury is ordinarily paired with 'thinking', probably because of its airy connotations, it is not equivalent to 'being' in the Cartesian sense; although it may appear to be so when Mercury tenants the same sign as the Sun. Mercury by itself has no jurisdiction over the 'I' or ego principle, though when it shares the same zodiacal position as the Sun, the chief objectives of the latter become indistinguishable from those suggested by Mercury's presentation. Mercury introduces thought for the Sun, but it is not thought itself. Although Mercury services the 'I' — the ego, represented by the Sun, the Moon and Saturn — it in no way defines it.

Descartes's conclusions make a lot of sense when understood in the light of his stellium in Aries, the reputed ego-maniac of the zodiac. Certainly, Aries' position as the first of the signs reflects its vitality and its sympathy for merely 'being'. Furthermore, Aries' symbolic connection with the brain adds fuel to an already 'heady' line-up of planets which indicates exceptional intelligence: the Sun, Jupiter, Uranus, Pluto and Mercury are all in Aries. All but Mercury form conjunctions to one another; however, Mercury's extreme receptivity would carry their collective force. Descartes's birth time is questioned, so the house placements and Moon degree are dubious, though Mercury does form a trine to sober Saturn, a weak conjunction to Venus and probably also to the Moon in Taurus.

In terms of zodiac position, his Mercury falls at the twenty-ninth degree of Aries, between two clusters of planets, one composed of the very strong 'mind' generators in Aries and the other of earthy 'body' planets in Taurus. It seems fitting that the great mind who spent a lifetime articulating and refining his thoughts on the mind/body split should have had his vehicle of expression, Mercury, straddling the cusp formed by the sign allocated to the brain and that associated with physical substance.

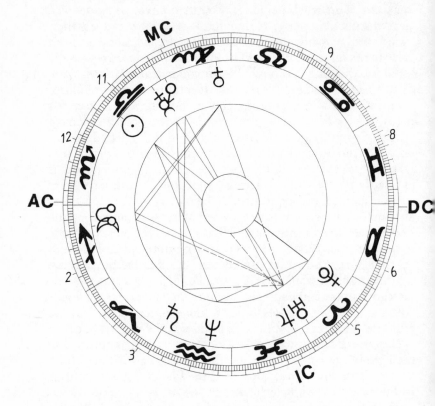

Figure 11 The horoscope chart of Friedrich Nietzsche.

His sombre message finds an echo in the caustic cries of Nietzsche: nowhere in contemporary philosophy do we find alienation so critically expressed. For moderns who espouse reason over faith or what Nietzsche called the 'herd instinct', the human condition is a bloodbath reeking of uncertain dreads, a web of false prophets. Nietzsche's horoscope is an ace example of how ambivalent aspect structure may colour an entire philosophy. His chart is that of a brilliant but tortured mind, one which is stricken by the extremist tendency to compartmentalize experience. Ambivalence aspects, oppositions linked by trine and sextile, constellate vast sums of energy, especially when comprised of Sun-Pluto, Mercury-Uranus and Mars-Jupiter oppositions. Tension resides in the opposition; repose falls within the trine-sextile mixture. Nietzsche's 'will to be' wages constant war against the dropout, ascetic sheep motivation with which Saturn-Neptune counters the triple-voltage oppositions.

This man's volte-face concerning his religious belief and heritage is characterized by the ambivalent structures' pendulum effect but also by that implied by the Sun, Moon and Saturn out of aspect to one another. These ego planets out of touch with one another incite the rebellious streak, along with the urge for originality. His family had always assumed that he would follow in his father's footsteps by becoming a Lutheran minister: to their consternation, he abandoned the study of religion for another field altogether. [2] Duality, Mercury's aide-de-camp, thrives on the see-saw effect that ambivalence patterns foster. The Sun's imprint here assures Mercury that knowledge is its primary objective and is pivotal to self-mastery and the Plutonian Sun guarantees that the subject's mental efforts would reach superhuman proportions. Sun opposition Pluto is the intelligence's wholesale conclusion that the father deity is fallible, if not corrupt. This Sun-Pluto combination implies a massive indignation, a rage and helplessness that follow the irrevocable discovery that the Father is mortal. The revelation that the Deity is a demi-god, if even that, is profoundly disappointing and one which stirs Sun-Pluto's compensatory superiority complex. Such individuals experience death as rape; to them it is the ultimate intruder and quite irresistible. They sense death's curious omniscience and for this reason secretly covet its power. The solution they raise is that of conquering death by actually inviting it. This may involve suicide — either literal or symbolic — or an outright rejection of any previous identification with a person or belief. It was doubtless the fact that Nietzsche lost his human father when he was only five years old that led him to reject the notion of a heavenly one. The death of the human being inspired in him such intense hostility towards the dead parent who had 'rejected' him that he felt obliged to reject in turn the religion to which that man had been committed and in later life to break his attachment to a stand-in 'God' or 'father', namely Richard Wagner.

Mercury's message inside Nietzsche's force field is: 'If God is dead, everything is possible.' Mercury's high profile on Nietzsche's midheaven suggests the view that there are no absolute values, no

divine commandments. Its Libra position in taut opposition to
Uranus invokes the unpardonable questions, the challenges to social
convention and yet the bondage of being trapped by society's claws.
Elevated Mercury makes Nietzsche a supremely skilled
communicator. He is a master aphorist and a king of wordplay;
incidentally, it is Mercury's love of words that accounts for this man's
early interest in philology.

Ironically, perhaps, it was Nietzsche's noble and life-affirming
attempt to uproot all manner of moral prejudice that, ironically,
accelerated his progress towards death. His intellectual arrogance
imposed a barrier between his solar and lunar consciousness. This
impasse bred the very thing he feared most: the 'monstrous and
frightening masks' which arose from the unconscious. Nietzsche's
disparaging of the physical, in particular of its feminine aspect,
undermined what was otherwise a towering achievement. His
audacity included the deliberate seeking out of sexual experience
with a syphilitic prostitute; it was as if he were daring the gods to
make him die. The manner of this conscious or unconscious
exposure to slow mental deterioration suggests that for him feminine
values equalled penance. The only conclusion that was possible
was a full-scale immersion in his intellect's opposite: complete
insanity.

Spiritual battles of the sort waged by Nietzsche are made even
harder to win on account of rising Moon positions. The Moon's
location in the first house is indicative of the needy, infantile
personality who escapes notice through adopting the role of supreme
observer. The Moon ascendant area suggests that human contact
is desired, but at arm's length. Unless the Moon makes aspects across
the horizon, the individual will feel inhibited, utterly self-conscious
and not at all inclined to engage the interest of others. The condition
simulates that of the infant who as yet simply gurgles, unable to
make successful demands on the world. For such a child everything
happens within a very limited field, the perspective being one of
total self-absorption and resistant to intrusion by others; Nietzsche
was evidently most uncomfortable in the company of strangers.
The outside world often sees those with the Moon ascendant as
snobbish and moody, when in reality the situation entails acute
timidity. This Moon placement senses atmosphere and can suss
out character mainly in its role as watchman: this probably accounts
for its prominence among the Gauquelins' *Writers* sample. [3]

Nietzsche, according to Freud, 'was more knowledgeable of
himself than any living man and probably anyone to come'. His

brutal self-honesty permitted him to confess: 'The thought of suicide is powerful comfort: it helps one through many a dreadful night.' His genius, had it survived the ravages of self-induced insanity, might have returned full circle. A fair proportion of his working life had been spent bordering the frontiers of a great truth; that he should have collapsed at the precipice before forging a bridge between faith and despair is the stuff of utter tragedy. Fortunately, for most of us, the level of duality Nietzsche experienced is altogether foreign. There are also others who exist within the framework of a comfortable faith which gives them a sense of permanence and gives their lives meaning.

Although Nietzsche's psychic tightrope act has since become altogether acceptable in certain realms, a more fashionable way of coping with one's uncertainty in relation to the world is by making a virtue out of it. This is to become divinely indifferent, 'not there' or, perhaps, merely empty: a stance adopted by Andy Warhol, the pop artist and underground film maker of the sixties. Of a world dominated by the allure of the ordinary, Warhol entranced his fans with his Campbell's soup cans and Brillo pad boxes, bewitched them by answering 'Yes' by 'No', 'No' by 'Yes' and sometimes by 'Maybe'. The danger of equating awareness with being becomes only too apparent when one inhabits Warhol's world: the conscious mind drifts into such peculiar places.[4] Drugs amplified Warhol's perception and his capacity to lift the banal above its station. The Uranus-Pluto conjunction in Virgo during the mid-sixties provided him with the necessary impetus to start a revolution within the commonplace. Warhol's birth certificate gives no birth time, only the date and place: October 28, 1930 in Forest City, Pennsylvania. Mercury makes a wide conjunction with the Sun from Libra and a possible square to the Moon. Warhol's Mercury has an unaspected quality in that his speech is somewhat equivocal, elusive. The loose Moon-Mercury square (which might not be present) would account for his role as a media celebrity, not to mention his preference for mundane, functional objects. Ronald Davison describes wide aspects as 'degrees of freedom',[5] and Warhol's Mercury certainly approximates that condition. The Libra placement of Mercury seems ridiculously apt when we consider Warhol's reputation for 'Yes, No, Yes, Maybe' responses. Warhol raises the provisional to the status of an art form. The work, however decadent, aligns form with substance. Mercury, through Warhol's hand, invokes Marshall McCluhan's famous dictum: 'The medium is the message'. As Oscar Wilde said, 'To expect the unexpected shows a thoroughly modern intellect.'

Andy Warhol's Birth Data as given in photograph of his birth certificate found in Edie: An American Biography, by Jean Stein and George Plimpton. October 28, 1930 Forest City, Pennsylvania. Birth time unknown. (Midnight positions used)

Sun 5 Scorpio 3	Moon 3 Aquarius 3
Mercury 29 Libra 20	Venus 7 Sagittarius 5
Mars 3 Leo 57	Jupiter 20 Cancer 21
Saturn 7 Capricorn 10	Uranus 12 Aries 32 ℞
Neptune 5 Virgo 20	Pluto 20 Cancer 53 ℞

Table 6   Horoscope data for Andy Warhol.

The three charts we have just studied were perhaps extreme examples, yet each in its own way spoke of the peculiar malaise that is prevalent in contemporary society. Most of us assuage our philosophical rumblings by choosing suitable distractions: tinkering with a computer or working in the garden does help to alleviate the unpredictable outcome of idle hands and an insufferable mind. The same Mercury that embraces angst is the first to forget it on the golf course, in the pub or at the hairdresser's. Evasion of this kind is justifiable, even constructive; provided it does not form the basis of an entire ethic: technology on a *grand* scale risks just that. The 'ghost in the machine' has long been Mercury's ally. [6] As long as technology produces bigger and better machines, no one need challenge Mercury's initial premise that a proliferation of objects (choices) is central to the concept of freedom. Technology supports Mercury's misguided notion that more is better and that external solutions are necessarily better ones (Band-aid theory). The logical consequences of technological overkill are a kind of modern *maya:* forms fool us, and their perpetrator, Mercury, would be the first to admit this.

Fortunately, not all the exponents of Mercury's emphasis on form leave us quite so forlorn; there are forms whose purpose is to uplift and enchant us by their mere beauty, and a notable example is art. Mercury's aesthetic influence is observed mainly in craft and technique; it shapes the method as well as the medium an artist chooses. Remember that Mercury is a funnel of creativity, not a source of it. Mercury is inherently didactic, a natural teacher. It sometimes represents learnt or acquired skills, often taken from set formulae; at other times, it operates by trial and error. It is unusually versatile. Mercury construction may be both novel and adaptable:

it can be quite original stylistically provided its source material, the rest of the horoscope, is sufficiently fertile. Most people think of Mercury as an imitator or copycat, but it might be described more accurately as either imitating or being imitated — there is really no middle ground. When Mercury's support system lacks sparkle, it will usually partake of the resources of its comrades, but if its back-up is a stellar treasure house, then Mercury itself will play the pied piper.

Mercurial art is distinctly modern, both in theme (alienation, despair; time/space distortion; futurism) and composition (simplification of line/form; construction). It is often an exercise in technique, more a test of craft than of genius. The content may be ambiguous, insular, altogether academic; or it may on occasion seem frivolous, cartoon-like mocking. The range of these effects is seen to best advantage in the work of Paul Klee, who, like Mercury, saw man as a 'prisoner half-borne on wings'.[7]

The work of this artist and academic represents 'the meeting place between the figurative and abstract'.[8] Technically brilliant, innovative and fanciful, his contribution epitomizes all that is Mercury. Where this is most obvious is in his choice of subject matter: masks and disguises, signs and symbols, childlike scrawls, schizophrenic imagery, geometric patterns and restless, distraught human figures. The impact of Mercury is seen elsewhere, in Klee's unusual variety — his output was 3,000 drawings and 200 paintings annually — and in his preference for working on a comparatively small scale. Typically Mercurial is his later habit of combining language (title) and image directly on canvas, a good illustration of this being *The Twittering Machine*.

The first impression one gets of Klee's horoscope is its incredible intricacy, which is in itself significant. Charts of this degree of complexity may signify either 'much ado about nothing' or the ingredients of genius. Judging which of the two extremes is at work is a subtle business, the key question being whether the aspects form a cohesive overall picture or are organized haphazardly. 'Much ado about nothing' occurs when too much is going on in a horoscope simultaneously. Unless aspects hang together reasonably well, too many aspects jam the Mercury circuits. The aspect-laden horoscope challenges Mercury's capacity to extract melody from the noise, a bit of routine alchemy that is not all that easy. What, then, of Klee's set-up? How does his complicated structure tax Mercury? Klee's chart, while complex, is unusually well integrated; notice, for example, the pyramid structure embedded in the overall pattern.

(Trace the following aspect lines: Uranus-Venus-Mercury-Saturn-Neptune-Uranus.) This infrequent combination points to stability and learning power; it also suggests an affinity with the mysteries a state of being attuned to the unknown. The presence of a pyramid shows both groundedness and experimentation: a respect for tradition and a capacity to take risks. While Klee's motiv⸱tion remains one of growth and acquisition, his chart allows for a variation in the approach and delivery of these goals. Strength resides in the flexibility of the structure, as denoted by the multiple kinds of aspect patterns, and in the sheer amount of space that the various aspects take up — there are no 'holes' or leaks in this chart. Mercury is thus anchored by consistent signals and there is

Figure 12   The horoscope chart of Paul Klee.

very little wasted interaction between it and its mentors.

That Klee was a supremely able and gifted communicator is evident from Mercury's inherent power around eleven degrees of Sagittarius and its position on the 'talent bank', the second cusp. He valued knowledge and placed a high priority on technical expertise in the realm of art. His view that man remains earthbound only because he has to is profoundly Sagittarian, especially within the context of a seond-house obligation. His work *The Hero with One Wing* depicts this sensibility.

That Klee's resolution of the modern struggle should have proved such a fertile one brings us to another story. Let us consider his chart again. According to Marc Edmund Jones's criteria, this horoscope would be termed a locomotive. The amount of energy it depicts is staggering, as is the potential for using it. The planets rise up and across the circle, making the perspective both broad and deep: Klee's interests are universal. Notice, too, that his map has no fewer than eight aspect patterns, with Mercury occupying five of them: in a word, the substance and tools are present for great accomplishment. The location of this planet within a seeker figure emphasizes Klee's natural idealism, his commitment to the search, while the T-square between Mercury-Jupiter-Uranus grants mental economy and an admiration for the avant-garde: there is no shortage of learning or of creative pressure here. The irritation combination made up of Venus-Mercury-Mars-Neptune seems particularly apt for an artist whose attention in his early years was consumed by the war between the sexes. The dominant triangle comprised of Mercury-Uranus-Saturn accounts for the formidable contribution he made to the realms of draughtsmanship and artistic technique. Mercury-Saturn links favour drawing ability, while Uranus allows the power of innovation full rein.

We see, then, that Klee's *oeuvre* is of especial interest to the student of Mercury. His etchings and paintings offer direct access to the hand of Mercury, while his writings on technique provide an insight into its purely academic side. At the beginning of this chapter I spoke of the importance of choice and its relevance to modern thinking. Before closing, let us consider something that Klee once wrote: 'The purest form of movement, the cosmic form, arises from the elimination of gravity, of our bond with earth.' [10] For him, it was entrapment that posed the greatest threat; yet flight was no resolution either. Instead, he chose art, for within the context of creativity he found freedom — and his spirit soared. We turn now from the Mercurial theme of modern conflict to another offshoot of its enigmatic ways, namely the worship of youth.

Figure 13 'Hero with One Wing', Paul Klee, 1905.
© COSMOPRESS, Genève and ADAGP, Paris, 1985.

Figure 14 'The Springer', Paul Klee, 1930.
                © COSMOPRESS, Geneve and ADAGP, Paris, 1985.

Notes

1. René Descartes, *Descartes: Philosophical Writings,* selected
   and translated by Norman Kemp Smith (Modern Library
   edition, 1958). See Descartes' discussion of the nature of mind
   and body in 'Meditations VI'.
2. Ronald Hayman, *Nietzsche: A Critical Life* (Quartet Books,
   London, 1981). The biographical material was extracted from
   this source.
3. M. and F. Gauquelin, *Writers and Journalists* (1970-71).
4. Jean Stein and George Plimpton, *Edie: An American
   Biography,* (Knopf, New York, 1982). This book on Warhol's
   chum Edie Segwick offers the reader a useful glimpse into the

world of Brillo boxes, etc. Just as the book reaches galley stages, I find Andy Warhol's birth data given elsewhere as August 8, 1931. The astrological conundrum and Mercury twist is that Mercury in both instances forms squares to the Moon. The August 8 date places the Moon in Gemini and Mercury in Virgo. Andy Warhol's 'as-if' universe continues right up through this book. No one seems to agree which birthday he prefers.

5. Ronald Davison. Personal communication citing Marc Edmund Jones.
6. Arthur Koestler, *The Ghost in the Machine* (Macmillan, 1967). A brilliant critique of behaviourist psychology's dehumanizing spirit. Essential reading for aspects of modern pespective.
7. J. E. Muller, *Magic Squares* (Methuen, London, 1957).
8. Margaret Plant, *Paul Klee: Figures and Faces* (Thames and Hudson, London, 1978). Biographical details plus art criticism found here.
9. Marc Edmund Jones, *The Guide to Horoscope Interpretation* (Theosophical Publishing, 1941). A classic work on horoscope shapings.
10. Plant, *Paul Klee,* p.66.

5.
Forever Young

May your hands always be busy
May your feet always be swift
May you have a strong foundation
When the winds of changes shift
May your heart always be joyful
May your song always be sung
May you stay forever young.
    Bob Dylan, 'Forever Young' [1]

The soul is born old, but grows young.
That is the comedy of life. The body is
born young and grows old. That is life's tragedy. [2]
                         Oscar Wilde

Mercury's leap from indifferent virtue to unmistakable decadence is caused by its inherent narcissism, a term which is used here in its broadest sense. Narcissistic behaviour, whether conscious or unconscious, is that which is fundamentally puerile, egocentric and resistant to change. Its basic assumption is that one is unique, special and deserving of continuous praise. A corollary of this belief is that time stands still and one's body is invincible — in effect, spared the ravages of the ageing process. Narcissists ensure the prolongation of their beauty by pampering themselves with potions and creams and by exacting flattery from their immediate surroundings. Equally characteristic of the narcissist is the feeling that one is the focal point around which events turn and to judge situations accordingly. Childhood allows the ego this type of indulgence, but maturity asks one to apprehend that the world is not designed for one's exclusive benefit. A third conviction common amongst narcissists is that one is exempt from the ordinary moral and legal strictures that might interfere with one's best-laid plans.

Narcissism is egoism in varying degrees, peppered by an erotic interest in one's own body. It implies youth in full bloom destined to die, as did Narcissus, for the love of his own image; and it means vanity, pretension and masterful role-playing. The common denominator throughout the range of its manifestations is the personality's infantility, its peculiar form of self-absorption. Feedback, however real or illusory, never quite registers: it remains vague, unsubstantiated, trapped by a looking-glass war. Self-adulation of this order spells gloom, for beneath the calculated insouciance, lurks an irrepressible sadness. Extreme, narcissism may incorporate the kind of hysterical or obsessive, compulsive traits which are ordinarily deemed neurotic. While narcissism is not necessarily neurotic and is in fact in small doses both healthy and desirable, it is true to say that neuroses usually thrive on a narcissistic element: that is, the psyche refuses for its own reasons to ripen beyond puberty. Dally comments: 'An inability to love anyone other than oneself can be regarded as a morbid streak since it makes a mockery of close relationships, distorts reaction to discontent and limits the possibilities of imaginative capability.' [3]

A narcissism that is out of control is distinctly morbid; it is the epitome of that fine malaise which is the earmark of Mercury. Within every narcissist lies an extreme dependence on the appearance of things and the tacit approval of the absent other, notably the mother. The mother here is characterized by a blend of perfectionism, rigidity, ambition, usually high intelligence and the inclination for emotional blackmail. Her affection is qualified, in that her love gets meted out like lollipops for good behaviour or extra hugs for star report cards. She is apt to be uncommunicative, notably with regard to physical or sexual matters, or absurdly conscientious to the extent that she might, say, dump appropriate literature on her child's desk at the first sign of impending puberty; thus she can never be accused of forsaking her maternal duty and responsibility. The key factor in the situation is that the relationship between the narcissist and his or her mother is held at arm's length, yet studded with mutual admiration. Narcissists speak very highly of their mother's beauty, abilities, charm, etc., but betray themselves by coupling this with pointed gibes about their mother's repeated failure in relationships or her emotional inaccessibility. Narcissism may also be a rather civilized, albeit passive way of denouncing authority. It may disguise a hostility towards any and all forms of authority. Witness the precocious teenager whose cocky impertinent remarks match those of even the most seasoned egotist's repertoire: an aversion for authority, a pretense of cooperation, petulance and an overdose of *amour-propre*. Conceit, an 'I' problem of the permanent adolescent, is specifically mercurial.

The astrologer might argue with some justification that Venus, not Mercury rules narcissism because it falls under the general category of beauty or dressing room vanities. Yet narcissism is not just a looking glass war. It also pertains to an absence of relationship in any truly meaningful sense. The narcissist feigns self-sufficiency but rarely obtains it. This is especially obvious when through force of circumstance, the narcissist is without person or hand mirror to define him. Being 'alone' is deeply threatening for someone whose sense of equanimity derives from constant feedback. And yet, even when the narcissist has the benefit of the multitude on whom he may bounce his reflection, he remains curiously estranged from himself and others. Any minor social triumph gained is offset by a hellish need to keep on winning approval . . .

The French existentialist playwright Jean-Paul Sartre understood that trap. His play *No Exit* introduces a female narcissist and mercurial type who despairs on finding no mirrors in hell and is thus obliged to use another character's eyes in order to apply her lipstick. [4]

Space limitations prevent me from elaborating on all forms of narcissism. Here we will focus on the most obvious variety, namely the physical. Because narcissism is primarily passive activity arising from a strong feminine influence on Mercury, we shall look carefully at the feminine hierarchy Venus, Saturn and Uranus. However, before proceeding in depth, let's examine four astrological factors which contribute to excessive narcissism.

1. Evidence of a shaky ego either through weak aspect pattern or weak personality planets (Sun, Moon or Saturn).
2. A clustering of planets in or around the eastern or western horizon.
3. An emphasis of one or more of the feminine planets (Venus, Saturn or Uranus).
4. An exceptionally volatile Mercury as shown by angularity, close aspect etc. Mercury need not aspect one of the feminine planets directly but it must be strong. As Mercury is the eyes and ears of the horoscope, it registers all signals quite freely of direct contact.

Notice that Saturn's exaggerated strength or weakness increases the probability of narcissistic underpinnings.

Physical Narcissism: Venus, Saturn and Uranus

The common or garden variety of narcissism turns up in the locker room. This may entail abject terror at the sight of the first wrinkle or an exaggerated watchfulness where the body's daily doings are concerned. Such vigilance may be very generalized or quite specific: the chart is not very helpful when it comes to isolating the particulars. However, one can start by considering the obvious. Body awareness begins at birth and is later supplemented by the mother/child interaction. Signals (Mercury) transmitted by the Mother (Saturn) to the child about the body (Saturn) are the most important factors in later physical obsessions. The body hierarchy includes Saturn, Venus and Uranus. Saturn provides the skin, the limits between one's body and the world; it also gives a sense of weight, purpose, physical solidity in space. Venus develops the sense of pleasure and gratification. Uranus liberates the body's ordinary awareness. It may accelerate nervous tension in the body as well as introduce newfangled protection schemes for it. Uranus likewise may stimulate bizarre bodily appetites.

Mercury Venus

Mercury Venus narcissism can be the standard bit of fluff one comes to expect at the beauty parlour. Poetry it is not. Both men and women of Mercury Venus persuasion banter about the esoteric properties of Vitamin E or the adverse effects of perms on split ends. But keeping well coiffed is only half the equation.

Mercury Venus gushes the way school girls and greetings cards do around the holiday season. Even Scarlett O'Hara's coquetteries border on sheer eloquence in comparison. Absent other input, Mercury Venus is fundamentally insipid. While there is admittedly something rather lazy about the mind that prefers the 'canned' sentiments of ad writers over those of its own making, the more inspired do-it-yourself poets are not much better. Romance is Mercury Venus's consuming interest. It wants above all else to be liked and in particular loved by a steady throng of admirers. The dead giveaway of a narcissist is his inability to sustain eye contact. Mercury takes the eyes thither and yon as if someone vastly more intriguing might loom on the horizon momentarily. The quest for feedback forces Mercury and Venus to fish for compliments: ('What a lovely dress!' — 'O', this *old* thing? I've had it for years: it makes me look perfectly awful.') False modesty and baiting for more approval is typical Mercury/Venus fare. Together Mercury and Venus can be silly and dilettantish. Whatever agenda the two planets dream up, romance is usually undermined by Mercury's restless, non-committal streak. In short, the curtain drops when the narcissist's engaging manner turns into a blank stare. Then the pact with another person, if any, is with illusion.

Artists recognized Mercury's ambivalence about ageing and thus portrayed him in two guises: the youthful winged god and the bearded sage. Angular Mercury in a natal chart usually coincides with a lean, gamin appearance; individuals with strong Mercury or Gemini usually look much younger than their chronological age. By contrast, Saturn ages the physical appearance. Curiously, both Mercury and Saturn males tend to have beards: the former liking them because of the illusion they create of greater age, the latter seemingly using them as props or handrests. Gemini rising and, to a lesser extent, Virgo rising may share the planet's elfin features and androgynous body type, provided there is no lunar interference which will cause a rounding of the body's proportions.

The best example of Mercury-Venus-Uranus influenced narcissism I have is that of a person who occupied the same house I did for several months. The advantage of living in close quarters with strangers with whom there is neither intimate nor familial bond is that one may observe first hand their idiosyncrasies with comparatively little distortion. One observation stuck in particular. Apart from clothes the only *personal* objects that he brought into the living space were a tiny Victorian reproduction night stand and a modern full length mirror.

The horoscope is a private one so I won't include a map or birth details. I'll summarize the astrological features quickly. The male has a disjointed aspect pattern which tilts to the left (11th, 12th and 1st houses) giving him an on-and-of-again social drive. He needs people around him constantly but on his own terms. For example, he won't go to public places such as cinemas or restaurants by himself; yet, he is loathe to commit himself to any specific plans until the last minute.

The Sun's low point position at 0 degrees Virgo in 11th house remains outside the overall structure. The ego thus aspires to high society but rarely feels a part of it. The father was evidently of lofty social origins but left the mother and him very early in his life. There has been virtually no contact since.

Venus rises above the Libra ascendant bestowing fashionable appearance as well as an ingratiating manner that appeals to much

older women but is off-putting to his peers. Mercury and Uranus
form a precise conjunction in Leo in the 11th house and hook by
trine to Jupiter. However, they too exist outside the main chart
constellation. The vulnerable Sun uses Mercury-Uranus and Venus
for making grand entrances and sweeping, indefensible statements
which more often alienate rather than please his associates. When
socially embarassed or trying to hide anger, his voice shifts from
a quite distinctive, resonant tone to a breathless giggle. Once I heard
him call out in French to someone he'd seen before but never met.
Neither he nor the person spoken to were remotely foreign. Mercury
and Venus obviously wanted to sound impressive, but wound up
instead sounding affected.

Figure 15   'Hermes in Repose' Museo Nationale, Naples. Photograph
courtesy of British Library.

Figure 16 'Phokion' Vatican Statue / misnamed Hermes statue. Courtesy of Oxford University Press.

When asked about this peculiar verbal exchange, he shrugged his shoulders and asked what he might have done instead. While there was a hint of understanding that perhaps speaking French to a non-native might be a bit odd, he showed no appreciation of why he might have done so in the first place.

Narcissists are typically oblivious to the impact they have on others. In particular, the narcissist usually misreads other people's verbal and non-verbal behaviour in a light most favourable to himself. The narcissist also expends considerable energy framing and embroidering his story in order to elicit the best impression. Alternatively, Mercury Venus might focus on an acquaintance's skills or accomplishments in order to bolster the narcissist's own.

Figure 17 'Bird of Hermes' from Ripley Scrowle Ms Add 5025. Courtesy of British Library Manuscript Collection.

Friends are described as being very, verrry smart or verry, verrry nice. The reliance on surface impressions and love of hyperbole make the narcissist a somewhat unreliable judge of character.

The distressing feature about narcissists is the extent to which the private face and public face so often differ. The person who galavants about town tossing non sequiturs to an unappreciative audience may be at home docile, almost self-effacing. There the only evidence of self-absorption may appear in the medicine cabinet where lotions and tonics abound. Let's move now to more extreme forms of narcissism that accompany Saturn.

Nutrition fanatics are especially suspect of narcissistic tendencies. Rigorous diets which exclude a high proportion of the food enjoyed by the general population constitute brilliant examples of a Saturn dominated lifestyle. Saturn invents rules. It cites authority. And, it enjoys the subtle pleasure of refusal of those food substances ostensibly bad for the body. Part of the joy no doubt arises from the saturnine type's identification of eating habits with moral superiority. Hyperattention to everything one consumes may be self-defeating. Usually behind this barrage of physical asceticism, one finds a layer of life-long guilt and ravenous hunger.

Body builders are another type of narcissist inclined to extremes. Training one's physical apparatus to such a pitch that it dictates one's every waking moment is literally constraining and self-indulgent. The irony, is of course, that the body narcissists who opt for control accuse the others of sloth and self-indulgence, when in fact their own grunts and groans betray their own weakness in that area. The second variety of physical fitness experts are those whose bookshelves are the repositories of every known manual on, say, lifting weights. A reliance on books — authority, which is Saturn — for physical experience is rather like a ninety pound weakling being dazzled by those ads which promise muscle and a bite of the apple. The point is that Saturn is petrified of biting into the apple; it is compulsively and inextricably caught in a web of lust and panic about it. Saturn's abstractions concerning the way the body should be throttle pleasure: instead, the mind becomes tied up with perfecting the organism and with establishing a standard. It gets lost clocking time, keeping score, and if Neptune is active, daydreaming as compensation for an unsatisfactory sex life.

Auto-erotic pleasure is the godsend of the infant. For Mercury, it defines another way of experiencing autonomy. With it comes an attitude of defiance and one-upmanship on the world that shuns private exploration — that is, of course, provided mother and her substitute, the Church, don't clog the brain with assorted claims concerning the more unusual consequences of masturbation. Guilt is the bane of any developing sensuality, particularly that form which gasps at the uninhibited nature of inquisitive children. Saturn's intrusion into this realm can be unhelpful: it instils the idea that physical stimulation is wrong, if not sinful. It is from this first contact with the mother's spoken or unspoken 'No' that the Mercury-Saturn personality acquires its familiar ability to do exactly the same thing. Mercury-Saturn loves saying 'No' to everything: there is a heavy investment in the power of the negative and an unconscious retaliation towards the first person who uttered it. The qualities of being ultra-discriminating, exceedingly circumspect, overtly critical and slightly sanctimonious are all indications of a strong Mercury-Saturn bond. (If you haven't noticed this, try *agreeing* with a powerful Mercury-Saturn disposition: you will have taken the wind out of his or her sails. Part of the reason for this is that Mercury-Saturn enjoys having the last word; it relishes the sweet virtue of posing the impossible question. Unlike Mercury-Mars, who experiences a physical exhilaration in verbal warfare, Mercury-Saturn thrives on the cold war; it needs to say or at least hear nadah!)

The rejection and denial ploys characteristic of Mercury-Saturn form an important aspect of the narcissistic personality. Coexistent with the narcissist's secret resistance to authority — which in fact breeds a closet authoritarian — is an ambivalence about human contact. There is an apparent but superficial interest in forming relationships. An iron barrier falls between the self and the other, usually for what are paraded as 'good reasons'. Good reasons as far as Saturn is concerned probably means a fear of either loss or separation. The net result is that body narcissists (including some athletes) are really uptight: that is, the body holds itself rigid, becoming an uncomfortable suit of armour. This rigidity may affect the subject's physical experiences with other people.

A key factor in physical narcissism is oral control. There is either an apparent lack of control or an excess of it. This may centre around food intake (i.e. nutritionist, anorexic, severely obese) or on the way one sounds when speaking. The mother invariably plays an important role in eating habits, but less obvious is her direct impact on speech patterns, such as one's use of vocabulary, articulation and grammar. In both instances, it is the *strength of Saturn* (the mother's attention to and training of these activities) which dictates one's relative concern with oral needs. Saturn's force next to strong Mercury may deepen the voice, which, of course, gives it an authoritative edge. One paradox concerning Mercury-Saturn is its capacity to be either a veritable motor mouth or a silent type. Perpetual babbling represents one means of control; another is the kind an individual commands when he or she times their statements for maximum effect. The net result in both cases is vocal domination.

Three personal examples illustrate this point: one man with Mercury conjunct Saturn ruling the third house in Leo on the MC in sextile to Venus, Mars and Neptune distinguishes himself as a graphic designer (line drawings show an excellent Mercury-Saturn relationship). Mother, ambitious for son's acceptance into 'proper' English society had him take elocution lessons at an early age. Although the voice sounds uniformly upper-class, especially under such circumstances as telephone conversations, first meetings, etc., under stress it breaks into its native colloquialisms. This individual suffers from depression because he is unable to reconcile his real origins with his apparent ones; he is always being misplaced socially and misinterpreted because of the sound of his voice. He readily admits to preferring America because of its 'classless condition', yet he is often guilty of patronizing his American associates, particularly with respect to their 'colonial' vocabulary and accent.

Another instance is that of a thirty-year-old woman, a commodities broker whose commercial savvy and sales skill have taken her to the top of her profession. Mercury figures heavily in her chart, as it forms part of a grand cardinal square/cross with the Moon, Venus, Saturn and Uranus. Mercury's eleven-degree Aries position shows drive, arrogance and intelligence. Its location in the third house opposition, Saturn, indicates that the voice/speaking ability will be in some way controlling. Nothing came to light immediately during our consultation, but later she asked to use the telephone to call her mother and ask permission to stay out longer. That struck me as odd, particularly as the woman was clearly old enough to traipse about London before nine at night. However, what really stunned me was the abrupt shift in the tone of her voice that took place when she began speaking to her mother. The straightforward, no-nonsense Arian manner changed to a barely inaudible whine which cajoled and begged Mummy to allow her to stay out for dinner; the tone was babyish, sentimental and entirely that of a five-year-old pleading for another ten minutes in the toy store. The case was made even more interesting by the fact that the woman-child business executive was a virgin and quite naïve as far as sex education went. Yet she certainly managed to use her voice effectively in business, and it seemed that she did the same thing to elicit permission from her mother.

A third example is the chart of a man in his early thirties whose intellect, erudition and linguistic ability are self-evident. His Mercury forms an exact opposition to Saturn and a tight trine to Uranus. Saturn's position in the fifth is a sure sign that interests will be serious and pleasures academic: this is an excellent position for strategy games, such as bridge and chess. This person's mother had been particularly keen that all her children should show exceptional achievement. She had read dictionaries to her son, and he had also been taken to a psychiatrist early on in order to resolve the usual sibling quarrels. When asked what she did with the child, the mother replied she played chess with him. Staggered, the doctor pointed out at that age children ordinarily played Parcheesi. The mother then groaned and explained that her son was *already* beating her at chess. The man in question is the ultimate consumer, devouring food as well as knowledge. He greets the pastime of gourmet repasts with great pleasure, and there is also an element of fear which manifests as a tendency to stockpile or store vast amounts of food. This leads to the purchase of enormous supplies of groceries as well as to an unconscious desire to eat continually. The weight excess creates a certain degree of body consciousness, which in turn leads to self-consciousness and a need to dominate by oral means.

In all three cases a certain amount of loneliness was present. Each person revealed a pronounced insecurity in relation to the mother, particularly with regard to her approval. Relationships for all three were somewhat tainted by unresolved dependency issues. In addition, each bore the characteristic of being irrationally judgemental about certain things, things which invariably reflected the bias of the mother in question. A study of several cases shows how anorexia might fall into this category. One outstanding example is that of a pre-teenager who has Saturn angular on the IC in square to Mars in Gemini, conferring body consciousness. Mercury, which sits on the ninth cusp in opposition to the Moon, disposes Venus, Uranus and Pluto. Anorexia is heightened body awareness. Characteristic of young female teenagers, it is ostensibly connected with a reluctance to mature physically. What happens is that the individuals concerned either simply stop eating or eat very little food and then attempt to reject it by vomiting. One thing about the anorexic's behaviour is very obvious: it is controlling. It forces everyone else to take notice of the person's diminishing body; moreover, it issues an even more provocative demand, namely that everyone else should feed that person. This ambivalence regarding self-nurturance is connected directly to one's perceived experience in early childhood. If one felt rejected either emotionally or bodily, the response made is likely to be one of a similar ilk, taking the form of a rejection of the self and/or the punishment of those who punished originally; an alternative to these might be excessive nurturance.

This brings us the subjects of overeating, overspending and the indulgence of emotional whims. Saturn's nature and influence are transmitted by the mother. Her response to a child's sexuality — whether horror or disgust, embarassment or indifference, delight, or in that rare instance, acceptance — registers permanently. That such reactions generally transmit a significant emotional charge accounts for the singular persistence with which they linger into the present. (Apologies to Freud for short-circuiting one of his more astute observations about the nature of human repression!) Sexual hang-ups are not the only cause of psychological misery, but they are likely to be the only cause if one is steeped in body consciousness. The odds are increased if Saturn plays an inordinate role in the horoscope and Mercury is around to draw conclusions about the assorted 'shoulds' that the early environment communicates.

Having mentioned Freud, we might look briefly at his own horoscope. His data are disputed; however, most astrologers use Lois Rodden's reference,[6] which gives these as 6.30p.m. LMT on May 6, 1856 in Freiburg, Germany. No need to quibble with the houses; the important feature with reference to Freud's clear body/materialist view is that Saturn forms a tiny intelligence triangle with Mercury and Jupiter. (Mercury semi-sextiles Saturn and sextiles Jupiter, while Saturn squares Jupiter.) The Hubers describe this pattern as the academic learning combination, one that is particularly relevant for the scholar. Venus dovetails off the side of the map; it aspects Saturn by sextile and Mercury by semi-sextile. Uranus' location in Taurus (along with Sun and Pluto) amplifies the strong body consciousness theme. Saturn, Venus and Uranus are all in plain view. The fact that Pluto is equally prominent in the Rodden chart by its quincunx to Mars and angularity indicates that Freud's rank materialism was not accompanied by indolence. The quincunx marks the major points of adaptation in the chart: it highlights the problems that must be regenerated. The subject's blind spot was his reductionist interpretation of human conflict: that he could see only a sexual basis for most difficulties seems hardly surprising considering the rather pointed indicators present in his horoscope.

Athletes yield a different brand of narcissism bred of physical savvy and an aggressive set of mind. Their protracted adolescence is probably as much related to the rigours of training as it is to the astrological indicators, which mandate a strong Mars (strength), Saturn (discipline) and Mercury (agility, speed). The single-mindedness of athletes and their uncompromising edge is critical for success, but neither quality is conducive to an ease at forming relationships. Although the irascible child star's unsportsmanlike conduct may cause spectators to bristle, it betrays a fragile ego. Apart from having the usual excuse of being young and pressurized, athletes, especially superstars, are also plagued (or possibly blessed) by the possibility of having Mercury's impertinent streak. Thus, regardless of their chronological age, they may have an additional factor to deal with, namely Mercury's predisposition to tantrums. A good example of this is 'superbrat' John McEnroe and his reputed bad manners. No one doubts his exceptional skill, but some might query his tennis-court decorum. He was born at 9.30 p.m. GMT on 16 February 1959 at Wiesbaden, West Germany. [7] Suffice it to say that Mercury is strong as it forms a conjunction with the Sun from its position of alleged exaltation (Aquarius). It is backed up by a powerful mutable T-square which holds Mars in Gemini, in opposition to Jupiter and in a square to Pluto. The Moon is in conjunction with Mars, thus adding emotional force and an unpredictable temper. Saturn forms a quincunx to Mars and a trine to Pluto, giving punch and endurance to the boy wonder; the year he reaped such lousy press notices and a thorough scolding from the Wimbledon committee (*quel scandale!*) brought progressed Mercury to the quincunx of Neptune. Some athletes never grow up: they crystallize at some high point of outer development, such as winning a gold medal or world title. Regrettably, this usually happens in their early twenties, just at that moment when the psyche is at its most self-congratulatory. All this reinforces the Mercurial idea that youth is in some way deified.

Time threatens the less successful athlete, particularly the one whose mind and emotions remain relatively undeveloped. The ego structure may be ill-equipped to handle limitation and may compensate, either by bragging or by brooding over real or imagined grievances. A different kind of response is shown by the athlete who plays Don Juan, skirting the winner's circle in favour of night carousing. This individual gets gossip-page attention but shows up rather poorly on the scoreboard: here, the ego planets are probably ungrounded, leaving Mercury a free rein to be mischievous. Narcissism shifts from its socially valued form — who argues with the Olympic team's unabashed physical preoccupation? — to its hedonistic counterpart which inhabits the fringes of the sports world.

Built into Mercury's overblown attachment to a wrinkle-free existence is the *obvious* impossibility of such an idea: therein lies part of its allure. Like the gambler whose world depends on the unlikely jackpot, Mercury is rather fond of ignoring the odds. Because of its dangerous enthusiasm and uncertain immortality, Mercury loves playing the daredevil. It hides its inferiority complex under bluff and counterbluff. Tinkering with fate is its most usual tactic. Mercury defies death; it challenges its assumptions. Implicit in this approach is Mercury's private assumption that it is an exception to the rule in such matters. The horoscopes of thrill-seekers reveal Mercury's self-destructive component and also its incredible agility when it comes to playing dodgems with death. Racing drivers and stunt artists need a heavy dose of Mars before they take that many risks.

Risk-taking is not, of course, uniquely physical. The narcissist employs other means for self-destruction such as emotional daredevilry. Case in point: Oscar Wilde, the classic psychological gambler.

Oscar Wilde's chart reveals a blend of emotional and physical narcissism. The highly intricate aspect structure denotes a complex personality. The aspects stretch in all directions, showing universal tastes; most, however, rise vertically, emphasizing Wilde's staunch individuality. The four-sided figure (Moon-Saturn-Mercury-Neptune) dominates the chart but is disrupted by the linear Mars-Pluto (quincunx) which darts across the seeming stability. Four-sided patterns are conservative and security-seeking, and quincunxes, especially those which operate alone, are hardly protective; Venus' unaspected position at the bottom of the first house further testifies to unpredictable bouts of harmony and disharmony. Already one senses the discomfort and natural conflict which characterized Wilde's personality; his two chief desires, to be a social maverick and to be materially safe, undermine each other.

Mercury's criterion of unusual strength is easily met by its rulership of the AC, MC and placement on the third cusp. The

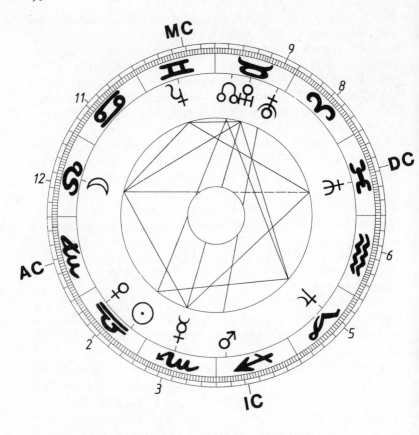

Figure 18   The horoscope chart of Oscar Wilde.

T-square configuration to Uranus and the Moon is amplified by
its location across mutable cusps. None of the ego planets are
particularly happy by hemisphere: the Moon straddles the twelfth
from the desperate pitch known as the cul-de-sac, the Sun is not
exactly shining below the horizon, and Saturn feels upside-down
on the midheaven. Thus, while each is reasonably well aspected,
none of them work best in their respective milieux. Saturn's MC
position, Uranus' tight opposition to Mercury and Venus' unreliable
noise all suggest physical narcissism. The Moon's vulnerable pre-
cuspal state augmented by Neptune's seventh house location add
stress, sensitivity and emotional insularity. Planets, especially the
Sun, Moon or Saturn, that tenant the area just before the twelfth

house, dance to a different drummer: the energy is at standstill. Individuals with the Moon here are undecided about their role in the world. Here rests the basis for a psychic tug of war between remaining in society (eleventh house) and submerging oneself in another world (twelfth house). Thus one is neither in nor out of the crowd, neither a social lion nor an outcast, and rests awkwardly and painfully in between.

Wilde's horoscope hangs on an agitated wit which espouses style, *joie de vivre* and a faint distress at the ordinary mortal's lack of pizazz. The classic dandy, Wilde explored narcissism both professionally and in his personal life. Selections from his writings show the extent of these themes and the carefree, jocular fashion in which he expresses them. His throwaway 'drop dead' lines are decidedly Mercurial. Consider the following:

'The only way to atone for being occasionally a little over-dressed is by being always absolutely over-educated.'[8]

'It is only the gods who taste of death. Apollo has passed away, but Hyacinthe, whom men say he slew, lives on. Nero and Narcissus are always with us.'[9]

Narcissism is, as we have seen, a state of mind associated with immaturity.

In recent years the press, echoing the sentiments of a youth-crazed public, have inundated the newstands with erotic photographs of pre-pubescent females. Cast at twelve in the role of a child prostitute, Brooke Shields is the archetypal example of a 'pretty baby'. The first actress to really capitalize on a pre-teenage sensuality, Shields has a horoscope which is the embodiment of physical narcissism. That she was catapulted to stardom and her beauty celebrated as the physical ideal is not at all surprising. The main part of the chart is organized around a mutable T-square. Gemini dominates the map, as it holds no fewer items than the Sun, Jupiter, the Moon, the node, Venus and the midheaven. The emphasis of Mercury in Taurus is even further substantiated, as it is the dispositor of all the Virgo planets and the ascendant. Saturn's sharp focus below the seventh house cusp indicates the power of the body consciousness as it stands by itself in Pisces in a square and in opposition to the rest of the planets. If one were to apply the traditional technique of mutual reception, Mercury would move to twenty-seven degrees Gemini and Venus to twenty-seven degrees Taurus, representing a kind of business trade-off with respect to beauty. Because Mercury is so powerful in the chart, as the ruler of the MC and AC as well as the dispositor of five planets, it is fitting that Shields should have acquired both the appellation 'pretty baby' and the title role in the film of the same name at the time when the progressed Sun and Mercury came to the conjunction of the midheaven and natal Moon. The resultant publicity swept the nation, and she remains very much in the public eye. Interestingly, her mother has been the major force behind all these activities.

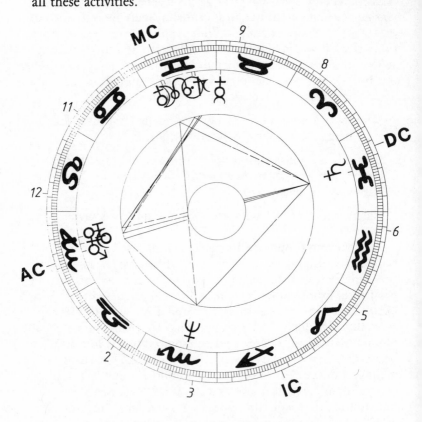

Figure 19   The horoscope chart of Brooke Shields.

The extremes to which West Coast fanatics will go in order to avoid the inevitable have had in some instances rather diabolical consequences, one example being the firm in youth-mad California that *was* in the business of freezing dead bodies. This firm, Cryonics

Interment Corporation Inc. began with good intentions: it operated on the theory that a person who died of a disease that was incurable today could be stored on ice to await revival in some future age when science would be able to cure it. Supported by the interest of numerous 'Cryonics Society' members throughout America, the Corporation, along with others, such as Trans-Time Inc., began collecting bodies in the late Sixties. As soon as a death certificate had been signed, the body was put on a heart or lung machine in order to maintain its circulation. Injections were given to prevent the clotting of the blood, which was subsequently drained off and replaced by a salt solution that protected the cells. The body was then put in a thermos-like capsule and exposed to liquid nitrogen, which initially lowered the body temperature to minus one hundred and ninety-six degrees Farenheit. The temperature was later reduced by a further hundred and fifty-four degrees Farenheit for the purpose of permanent storage. The fees for this type of suspended animation were not cheap: starting prices began around 25,000 dollars. However, one had the option of charging it to a credit card, in effect buying time on time — a thoroughly Scorpionic exercise that was described by one cynical reporter[10] as 'Pay now, live later.' (The fact is that quite a few people paid, but they certainly will not be living later.)

In January 1978, seven years after the State of California had suspended the corporation status of Cryonics Interment Corporation Inc. for undisclosed reasons, a scandal broke in Northern California when relatives of the company's deceased clients found the allegedly frozen bodies abandoned in an obscure building. Its President was sued for damages. Chasing representatives and facts about the case proved difficult: no one wanted to talk about it. Disillusioned company members had dispersed early on in the project. One ex-officer informed me that he had left in 1970, suspecting an impending bankruptcy and foul play. He refused to comment further, as he did not wish to taint the field of cryonics by further publicizing this most unfortunate outcome.

The most important ingredient in any horoscope, whether of a person or a corporation, is its relative coherence. Does the chart show clear or contradictory objectives? Are the incoming and outgoing signals strong or weak? It is the aspect structure which answers these questions. If the links between the planets are tenuous, due to wide aspects, then motivation lags and diffusion sets in. Loosely woven charts are tricky for both individuals and organizations; the latter, however, are far more vulnerable to flimsy aspect patterns for the simple reason that groups with ill-defined goals rarely get off the ground. Businesses, in particular, cannot sustain long-term successes without a clear, obvious strong motivation pattern. Experience with corporation charts demonstrates that group charts usually function at the level of mass mentality: the weaknesses will be much more difficult to overcome, as the free will of the masses is not that free.

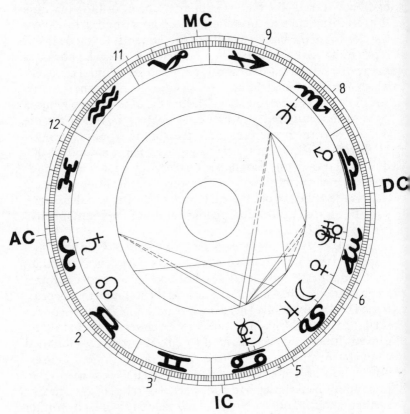

Figure 20 The horoscope chart of the Cryonics Corporation.

The critical element of the Cryonics Interment Chart is the number of weak aspects (dotted lines). Corporate purpose is diluted: communication inside and outside the firm will be distorted, possibly evasive. Distribution around the wheel shows a prominent north-western emphasis, revealing a dependence on others for success plus a potentially aggressive, manipulative streak as indicated by the weight of the fourth, fifth and sixth house planets. The Aries ascendant ruler, Mars, unaspected in the seventh house reiterates the possibility of imbalanced aggression. Specialized interests are shown by the Sun-Uranus-Neptune triangle: certainly, the Cryonics Interment Corporation held unusual, offbeat technological concerns. This is further substantiated by the little 'ear' figure made up of Sun, Moon and Uranus, which signals unorthodox sensitivities, an almost weathervane temperament. While the thrust of Cryonics Interment Corporation was ultimately destroyed by its unsavoury activities, its ostensible purpose and ideas represented progressive thinking. Little 'ears' serve as antennae to hear or see the trends of the future, thus it is not unlikely that the field of cryonics will blossom later, once the technology improves and the expense of the operation is reduced. The ego triad (Sun-Moon-Saturn) is held together by a wide aspect. This points to the tenacity which kept the company functional, albeit illegally, for seven years after its suspension. Saturn's angular placement and strong degree indicate that the physical world and its limitations will play an important role in the corporation's life; this also shows blocks and frustrations, and also, needless to say, the freezing temperatures necessary for storing the bodies. Appropriately, Mercury and the Sun square Saturn, highlighting intelligence and body consciousness; cryonics is concerned with the preservation of the body. Some might say it represents the height of narcissism and materialism.

Mercury's role as the commercial god is always relevant in business charts. Here it rules the third and sixth houses which are, of course, its own. It touches Saturn, Pluto and, by a weak trine, the planet Neptune. The Pluto tie is reasonable given the association with death or transformation of the body. Neptune's Mercury connection shows that the Cryonics group possess a lure that is persuasive, almost charismatic — Mercury-Neptune trines are typical of evangelists! Moon square Neptune is not a good business aspect: it suggests that follow-through is nil. Even the meticulous qualities of Mercury-Saturn rarely offset the weakening of attention which Moon-Neptune brings. The scandal surfaced in January 1978, when progressed Mercury retrograde turned direct. Transiting Pluto was squaring Mercury, transiting Neptune quincunxed Mercury and the progressed Moon opposed Mercury. Mercury's love of joy rides and its desire to dice with death are dealt with in another form in the next chapter.

That Mercury's idiosyncrasies should include narcissism is fairly straightforward. Yet what accounts for the recent surge of narcissism, above all in the West, as exemplified by body culture USA? Is this a sign that mankind is having a tantrum?, refusing to grow up? Does decadence reflect a massive *coup de pied* for the mother, church, school and state, or is it simply that Mercury's whorish ways applied on large scale acquire the values of those with the loudest mouth? Who, then, deserves categorical attack? Which nation bears the responsibility for shifting Western values? Which group by virtue of its temporal power holds the obligation to put away its toys? The media, the collective's Mercury, must bear the brunt of the criticism — but where is it that the media holds highest

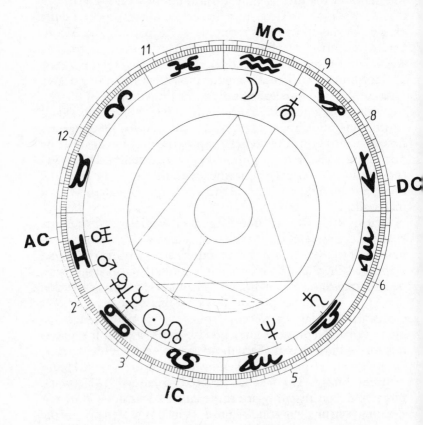

Figure 21   The horoscope chart for the United States of America.

court? Clearly in Mercury-ruled America.

The horoscope of the United States has been allotted different dates and a variety of Ascendants. I endorse the most common one, which gives a Gemini ascendant and an Aquarius midheaven. Nowhere else in the world are the cult of the young and the spirit of the underdog more openly championed, and variety is an American byword. (Who started the twenty-eight flavour ice cream fad? None other than Cancer stellium, Gemini ascendant America — kids' stuff!) Freedom of speech has long been an American obsession; and no other country compares in terms of broad-based communications, commercialization and transportation services. Narcissism is rampant in America. Body awareness is keen, as Saturn forms a tight square to the Sun. Health farms, gymnasiums, million-dollar sports, and the sales of cosmetics and athletic equipment all thrive on the open market. Part of the reason lies in the fact that the USA lives for spending. Also, it dotes on the young and seeks to prolong the period of youth by the performance of assorted rituals.

In America, exhibitionism has long been the sport of the West Coast: California, peacock country, boasts more film stars, health faddists and flagrant hedonists than any other state. Its horoscope reads like a cross between a Zen Buddhist and a hysterical two-year-old; it spells excitement, reform and innovative ideas. The aspect structure denotes a massive idealism and a deep-rooted instability, the chart's most outstanding feature being its five-planet irritation triangle (Moon-Venus, Uranus, Pluto and Jupiter). The nature of irritation patterns is to incite revolution. These aspect combinations (opposition, quincux and semi-sextile) are arousing, somewhat militant; in a natal chart such figures denote creativity plus a restless, hyper-reactive manner. The planets inhabiting the irritation triangle will show what kinds of issues the individual or collective will confront.

California's chart contains two such formations. The first one throws those comfort-loving home and family planets the Moon and Venus into a somewhat harsh, volcanic contact with Uranus, Pluto and Jupiter; thus Californians will experience somewhat sharp, uncomfortable domestic crises. Their views on family life will be progressive, and they will also hold a powerful and mysterious penchant for the transient and uprooted. The second irritation triangle is composed of the body narcissists Mercury and Saturn and the thinking contributor, the Sun: herein lies the essence of California's body ethic. It is where the Sun is brought into contact

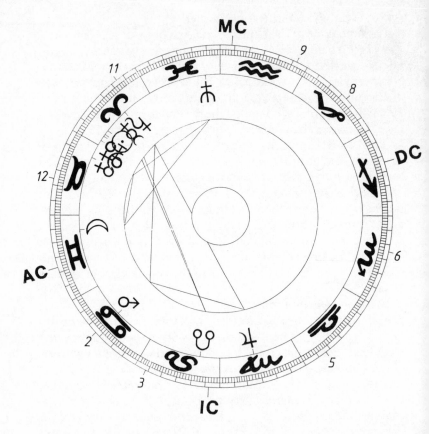

Figure 22   The horoscope chart of the State of California.

with the convictions of the body that the sun-worshippers *par excellence* are found: staying young thus becomes a point of ego, a measure of the will. And in California one does this best by witnessing one's true views: 'Why wouldn't you want to prolong life, save your lungs, contract your waistline, give up smoking, take up sunflower seeds?' California's Virgo Mercury takes over in a consummate fashion, organizing vitamins, minerals, cell salts, etc. Self-indulgence turns into hypochondria.

   One last point about California: the Mercury-Saturn-Sun trio has been instrumental in creating its lingo. If we recall that Mercury and Saturn relate to oral control, either through words or sound, it seems fitting that the state holding such a pattern should be the cornerstone of slang production and of such verbal *asanas* as 'space' and 'awesome'.

Notes

1. The title of this chapter was taken from Bob Dylan's popular song, recorded in 1973. Dylan's horoscope and lyrics are pure Mercury. Highly recommended listening and/or reading for those unfamiliar with life 'like a rolling stone'.
2. J. M. Stuart Young, *An Urning's Love* (Hermes Press, 1905).
3. Dally, *The Morbid Streak,* A good survey of various kinds of negative thinking and behaviour which often typify the unhappy Mercurial type.
4. Jean-Paul Sartre, *No Exit* (Vantage Books, 1955). This is a splendid play and one that feeds on Mercury's vanities and manner of evasion.
5. Huber threefold personality chart obtained from Huber teaching materials provided at various seminars.
6. Lois Rodden, *The American Book of Charts* (Astro Computing Service, 1980), p.
7. Birth data: 9.30 p.m. February 16, 1959 at Wiesbaden, West Germany, (*Astrological Lodge Quarterly,* Spring 1984).
8. Oscar Wilde, *Phrases and Philosophies for the Use of the Young* (Printed for private circulation, page 6).
9. Ibid.
10. Cryonics Interment Corporation Inc. (see p.87) quote by journalist.

6.
God of the One-Night Stand

Despite the notorious philandering of Zeus and company, Mercury/Hermes is rarely portrayed as being particularly amorous or even as the counterpart of a particular goddess; and yet his reputation sniffs of Dionysian revelry and debauchery. Apart from his infamous coupling with Aphrodite, from which came the monstrous hermaphrodite, Hermes seems more the loner, almost a celibate — so why the discrepancy? Mercury's bad press reached its acme in the scathing attack made on him by the Greek poet Hesiod.[1] Although Zeus created Pandora in revenge against Prometheus' importuning, Hermes was held responsible, according to Hesiod, for the wily defects of that seductress (and for those of women in general) as it was he who had bestowed Pandora with the gift of lies. Hermes was guilty, but only partially so: he was, after all, merely fulfilling the duties set out by Zeus. Thus Mercury, the public servant, winds up as the patron of seduction. His unsavoury image is not enhanced by the fact that he is a runner. He has become the mortar to the gossipmonger's pestle, the collective assumption being that if one runs, then it *must* be away from something odious — like responsibility.

Brief encounters are Mercury's forte, because he seeks diversity in numbers. His apparent licentiousness is really a production-line mentality: quantity beats quality. Mercury operates on the false premise that more is better; until, of course, he discovers the fact that *more* is simply the same. (*Plus ca change, plus c'est la même chose.*) The nature of the beast is to appear high-spirited when he really is rather predictable, curious and a clock-watcher. Mercury stands alone when it comes to cruising. He cases the territory and samples its wares, be they literary or erotic: the classic shopper! (It certainly wasn't Venus that went looking for Mr Goodbar — she would have stayed home in wait.) Mercury's open ogling of the naked Aphrodite when she and Eros lay trapped *in flagrante delicto* beneath Hephaestus' net is the mythical equivalent of latter-day voyeurism — harmless, if not rather pathetic. Peep-shows on Olympus could hardly have been as tawdry as are those staged in Soho yet both places seem to be peopled by ordinary types getting the odd charge from human anatomy.

Mercury's orientation is that of voyeur, of someone who stands outside experience and examines objects from afar. To him the world is composed of form, an alien substance that is without either history or consequence but merely is. The voyeur is subjective particular, so Mercury's view is unique, weighted on the side of the observer. It pans the horizon, accepting images as they arise and yet controlling them through the eye of the camera. Relationship is nonexistent and pleasure, no matter how carefully orchestrated, is transient; at a distance the erotic is flat and one-dimensional, very much like a waking dream, and subject to the whim of an uncertain lens. Behind whatever sexual ploy Mercury manifests lurks a need for the control of the environment, and within the sight-dominated sensuality it promotes pleasure and pain are intermingled. The Mercurial child is no less prurient, and, like adults, he resorts to euphemisms when it comes to naming of unmentionable subjects, such as the origin of babies; the ubiquitous white stork who absolves human beings from any direct responsibility for conception has a 'herald' status that suits Mercury. Childbirth, so it would seem, occurs thanks to a kind of celestial midwifery whereby babies become foundlings abandoned by the gods to the ways of men. Stork lore may be a cover-up, but it is one that is critical to the individual's early development, far from it the child learns that the substitution of one name for another imbues objects with a special significance: thus secrecy comes to be equated with power. In Mercury's heyday, namely the period between the ages of six and twelve, such absurd notions as that of the stork are eventually challenged; yet these ideas have their roots in magical thinking — and, as we shall see later, Western civilization has contrived to whitewash even the stork.

Mercury balances any paradoxical elements that may exist by veiling them in eroticism. Relationship, an essentially Venusian or lunar function, begins within the intimacy of the family, from which one acquires the 'feeling' values that are necessary for positive bonding and reasonable trust in other people. Loss or separation from the mother at an early age stunts this process: trust may be recouped, but not without a substantial time-lag and the probable intervention of Mercury's defence reaction, that of rationalizing emotions. School provides the individual's next chance to learn about relationship, but it is no panacea and its impersonal nature prevents it from being a cuddly mother substitute. What it does do is provide an appropriate launching pad for social experience, an area which falls entirely within the horoscope's third house. A close examination of this house shows not only how an individual interacts within small groups — in the classroom, for example — but also the degree to which the early environment influenced or modified his or her social attitudes. Broadly speaking, Mercury relates to the set of the mind and its receptivity to new kinds of endeavour. (A degree of receptivity is an obvious asset when the individual is confronted with the ordinary expectations associated with school.) It is also hitched to the social struggle whereby one stands among peers and negotiates familiarity. Both factors shape one's capacity to experiment, to indulge guilt-free and without fear in erotic adventure: the former implies a willingness to reach out to the world and the latter a certain degree of autonomy.

The problem is that Mercury's prime coincides with that time when school and family stimulate certain aspects of curiosity and quash others, in particular those regarding sex. Sexual attitudes are learnt, not inherited. Astrologically, they are house-related, the house in question being the third. The houses represent the environment from which one absorbs messages about the world. Third house signals are tradition-bound: their input is localized and parochial, inclined towards prejudice if not tunnel vision. Alas, youngsters of this age find school on the whole monotonous and conventional. If teachers treated sex as indifferently as they do arithmetic, its lure for the school student would be no greater than that of the multiplication table. When adults retain unresolved feelings where their own sexuality is concerned, sex remains a potent force for transmitting unconscious conflict. Such ambivalence becomes magnified within the third house, where information is best but is rarely passed on in an objective way. Yet education sharpens the critical faculty, thus enabling Mercury to overturn previous assumptions. How far Mercury strays from the collective value system depends on its strength in comparison with that of the third house. An exaggerated third house locates power in the milieu, so that the socio-cultural matrix overrides individual conviction. An errant Mercury is probably a strong one whose positive or negative expression is dependent on the other factors.

Third house constituents, siblings and schoolmates, strike the first chord of give and take, and from playground to clubhouse the young soon intuit one another's place in society. Perceptive but often cruel, children define the schoolyard pecking order by the use of names such as 'bully', 'wallflower' and 'egghead', acceptance or rejection by one's peers in early childhood is a third house phenomenon and one that is critical to group trust later on. Also pertinent to this house is one's sense of command or helplessness within the environment. Academic achievement fosters some control, while failure does the opposite. Communication, a major vector in academic success, is Mercury-linked. Reading and writing are insufficient in themselves: self-expression and the ability to *listen* are also vital. Third house factors (Mercury, planets in the third and the ruler of the third) show not only what one says and the way in which one proceeds to say it but also one's sense of timing and the appropriate setting for voicing personal opinions. It is my contention that effective communication skills underline all positive erotic experience: the ability to fully appreciate the other person presupposes a reasonable means of talking to him or her.

Stressed Mercury assaults its milieu with verbiage but is disinclined to notice the lousy impact that results. Individuals of this type are not word-shy; to the contrary, their handicap is that of dominating the floor, of speaking for other people (putting words into their mouths) and failing to listen. An equal hindrance is the obscurely placed Mercury or third house ruler. Here people have trouble articulating desires as well as getting others to pay attention to them. Typically, such individuals respond by resignation: 'Nobody ever listens to me, so why bother trying to express myself?' However, neither a very strong Mercury nor a weak one is quite as thorny as those cases where the power of the sign overwhelms planetary capacity. For example, charts with a lot of Gemini and, to a lesser extent, of Virgo — need a strong Mercury in order to accomodate the sign's input. Should Mercury have few aspects, the sign energy will have a limited number of outlets: the total effect is a build-up of inner tension which surfaces inappropriately now and then in the form of compulsive talking, *non-sequiturs,* extreme nervousness, heavy smoking, and so on. Such persons irritate their surroundings and are quite oblivious to the fact. Communication is hard enough among those people with relatively easy-going aspects to Mercury and the third house. When Mercury is unduly emphasized by either stress or a lack of it and the position is complicated by a weak aspect structure, communication benefits from instruction. Most communication blocks stem from poor listening habits: a strong Mercury needs to listen to others, while a weak Mercury needs to listen to itself. The third type needs to listen not only to itself but also to the outside world.

The way a teacher interacts with students in class will affect the way those students communicate among themselves. Ridicule by a teacher undermines a student's social confidence, as does isolation treatment. A humiliation, in the form of unfair criticism, or a caning before one's friends, makes an indelible impression on the psyche; acutely embarrassing school situations provide the building blocks for social outrage. The state of a child's map intimates whether his or her indignation is buried or ventilated, emotional events of this order generally being marked by progressions or transits to Mercury, to the third house and its planets and rulers. Because teachers are often the first contact a child has with 'social' justice, such experiences are major turning points in psychological development. A bit of astrological detective work can usually unlock the social fears rooted in educational blunder.

Upsets in the organism regarding trust and fair play are hardly conducive to easy relationship. The misuse of power by teachers or parents before one's contemporaries breeds a subtle contempt for hierarchical relationships (teacher-student, employer-employee, police-citizen). Should this disdain go unnoticed for too long, it is apt to return full measure in inappropriate circumstances, such as marriage, where equality is presumed but rarely practised. One-to-one relationships relive power struggles by means of a familiar manoeuvre: loss of privilege, usually sex. Cold wars are nothing more than communication 'freezes' whereby Mercury retaliates by creating two-way barriers. Women have long indulged in this ploy, mainly in reaction to extreme feelings of bondage and in some cases to a lack of freedom within marriage. The trend is shifting, and now men are manifesting a similar reaction physiologically: whereas formerly women simply begged off 'duty' through a series of excuses, men are now expressing their indignation in the form of impotence. Sexual difficulty in both the early and later stages of marriage is traditionally linked to problems of communication. Mercury is thus both the perpetrator of the pain and the potential implementer of recovery. When neither party is willing to relinquish his or her position, Mercury breaks the impasse through the wise adjudication of the healer and counsellor Thoth. For some, Thoth might represent prayer or a link-up with some form of higher guidance, while for others it may mean direct third-party intervention. Rising above such difficulties does not mean denying or ignoring them but rather inviting Mercury to stand high above the situation so as to enlighten and enrich the perspective of the individuals in question.

Mercury's erotic core builds on those patterns established just before puberty, when sexual characteristics remain undifferentiated. The period of androgyny, which lasts roughly from nine to eleven, corresponds to that time shortly after birth when the body is at its most shapeless and the experience of separation at its most acute. This, combined with Mercurial curiosity, leads the individual to explore anatomical differences in the company of siblings. The advent of puberty and its attendant stress obliges the jellyfish psyche to navigate the territory close to home; if brothers and sisters are lacking, neighbours and even adult relatives may conspire to provide surrogate partners in the discovery of pleasurable experience with members of either the opposite or the same sex. Playing 'doctor' is one way in which children role-model authority figures and justify what they might otherwise suspect to be an adult privilege. The phase passes with a blast of giggles until the arrival of adolescence, when sexual fulfilment assumes a disturbing urgency. When for some reason his sexual curiosity is either blunted or exacerbated by adult intrusion, Freud's polymorphous child is in for complications. Mercury's aspects reveal sexual vulnerability, particularly to incest. The highly Mercurial child is apt to be sexually precocious and more likely to be a *willing* rather than a *reluctant* participant in adult seduction. Furthermore, most sexual interference with children by adults occurs when the people concerned live in very close proximity, as in the case with neighbours or family, an area traditionally associated with the third house.

Venus, Mars and Pluto figure as contenders when it comes to the evaluation of potential sexual partners. If these three planets form hard aspects to one another in the parent/child synastry, they may trigger constant rows. Mixed with Mercury, the chances are that sexual manoeuvring has been in the air. That the sexual innuendo may never have been acted out is immaterial; though formally no breach of the law has been committed, the psyche's own law has been violated. Mercury registers contradictory signals, especially those of an erotic nature. The body and emotions will do likewise, converting excitement into a symptom, such as excessive urination or compulsive spending. The state of urgency and excitement is thus retained; missing are a sense of control over such reactions and an understanding of their origin. Therapeutic intervention calls on Mercury to reconstruct the process, to identify the connections that exist between present symptoms and the original messages stored in the mind, body or emotions. The symptoms present, whether mental, physical or emotional, are usually an offshoot of the personality's favourite reference point. (See Chapter 9 regarding the role of the Sun, the Moon and Saturn.)

Although Freud posited the view that seduction in childhood takes place more at the level of fantasy than at that of reality, I myself have heard too many client confessions from the adult end (concerning overt sexual tampering with their own children or that of neighbours or relatives) to be similarly convinced. It would seem that either the arrival of a more open, permissive society is letting people speak more frankly about acts of incest or that relaxed mores are actually leading to an increase in the number of such acts. It may also be that as an astrologer one attracts a more extreme population, one which is conceivably more experimental in its life style and behaviour — I don't know. Certainly, Freud's conviction regarding sexual fantasy appears to have an application that is far less universal than he originally surmised. What was of enormous benefit to mankind is his institution of the talking cure, of which Mercury is the supremo. (Freud's Mercury forms a precious little 'ear': Mercury semi-sextile Saturn, semi-sextile Venus. The Moon's Gemini location reiterates his belief in the value of psychoanalysis.)

Mercury's counterpart, Jupiter, may play an important role in incest. He, in the guise of 'Uncle' turned up more frequently in my files as instigator of child/adult sex play than anyone else. I make this statement cautiously, as it arises more out of a clinical hunch that from any substantial conclusion. Jupiter, the planet of sensory knowledge, may well be the true seducer. (I am prepared to believe that 'Uncle' may in some instances really be 'Father', but that clients were unable to bring themselves to admit that: 'Uncle' somehow holds less of a shock than 'Father'.) On Olympus, of course, Zeus/Jupiter assumed the role of God-cum-father over the other deities; he was, moreover, frankly charmed by the perversity of Hermes/Mercury. The reluctant party in the case of a seduction by relatives is usually trying to please or to win affection; willing family members experience guilt because they participated freely and enjoyed it. That the adult should be singled out for chastisement whereas they are not seems unfair to the children in question. The shy child reacts to the guilt imposed by larger institutions, such as the law and the Church: shame, plus fear of the possibility that he or she really was provocative, colour his or her reaction. Women who have been raped have been known to voice a similar ambivalence when seemingly put on trial by the public for offences committed against their own person.

The classic cudgel for hammering away at lust is God with a capital G. A brief stint as a token Protestant sex counsellor to an 'alternative' Catholic group taught me that guilt was the main reason humans suffer in sexual experience. This guilt is usually derived from some isolated occurrence of being caught with one's knickers askew. The most sophisticated of parishes are no more enlightened in such matters than are the fundamentalist ones: fire and brimstone may not be their poetry, but silence certainly is. The recent rash of 'liberated' books on sex written for children may have reduced the amount of unnecessary secrecy to a minimum, but unfortunately none ever tackles the more subtle issues of pleasure, intimacy and taboo. Liberated Mercury makes the error of assuming that the facts are enough.

Mercury-dominated eroticism is an amalgam of the following: auto-eroticism, cerebration, gamesmanship and anonymity. These traits may occur either in isolation or in combination with one another, the key element being a need for variety and impersonality. Although called bisexual, thus implying an equal attraction to both sexes, Mercury's attitude to either biological sex is more or less indifferent. The polarization, if any, lies towards the same sex, especially during those phases when the male meets his feminine aspect and the female encounters her masculine side. Mercury's androgynous character suggests an asexual attitude which leads it to shun the erotic tie in favour of the occasional mechanical or indifferent coupling. Any pleasure derived from either sex is fundamentally self-gratifying. The logical outcome of Mercury's cerebral style of behaviour is pornography: material which, devoid of 'feeling' values, titillates its viewers at the expense of female dignity. The bulk of such literature reveals aggressive components, not to mention deplorable taste. For the more literate consumer of pornography, sex becomes an abstraction, a philosophy in its own right; consider the following example.

That revolutionary ogre and eighteenth-century French libertine the Marquis de Sade still shocks the censors with his *Philosophy of the Boudoir,* which correlates sexual licence with social freedom. That Sade's aberrant logic should have allowed him unspeakable depravity in no way alters the fact that he made a major contribution to our modern understanding of one very significant aspect of human nature — sheer, unbridled egoism. Born into an aristocratic family, Sade was separated from his mother at an early age and sent to his uncle to receive an education.[3] His precocious manner was no doubt stimulated by the licentious ways of this relative: an intelligence of Sade's order (Sun-Jupiter conjunction in Gemini, Moon Virgo) distorted by utter selfishness and an environment of decadence is bound to be misused. The high mutability filtered through a Mercury-Uranus tie is certain to be unsettling, both to the subject and his associates.

Games, by convention, are elaborate rituals. Those inspired by Mercury require rules, role-playing and often a special language. These may include cross-dressing (wearing the apparel of the opposite sex). Games between two or more usually entail some division of labour and assignment of power; here Mercury displays a somewhat compulsive streak. The advantage of games is that the roles involved are predetermined and the outcome fairly limited. Mercury's aversion to nuance in human relationship is safeguarded by the fact that there are preset objectives. Within the contours of a game, the freedom to experiment is far greater; somehow the time limits and rules of play form a safety net within which risk taking can take place. Sade relished games: particularly his own, a kind of sexual roulette based on the element of surprise as to which guest got maimed.[4] In his parlour what was certain was that one player, if not a dozen, would lose. Whether cerebral or gamesman-like Mercury relies on control: without it, there is impotence — not necessarily sexual incapacitation, but rather a certain helplessness in the face of erotic options. The ugly aftermath of such helplessness is not unknown to raving psychopaths.

Marquis de Sade, June 2, 1740, Paris, France, 9.13 p.m. LMT (speculative). (Other times: 7.15 a.m. and 2.00 a.m.)

Sun 12 Gemini 28	Moon 15 Virgo 49
Mercury 18 Taurus 45	Venus 27 Cancer 27
Mars 24 Aries 45	Jupiter 17 Gemini 17
Saturn 22 Cancer 06	Uranus 13 Capricorn 51 rx
Neptune 4 Cancer 12	Pluto 6 Scorpio 06 rx

Table 7 Horoscope data for Marquis de Sade (Lois Rodden, *The American Book of Charts*).

The sex killer John Gacey is no exception. Once a pillar of the local community, his name fell into disrepute when he became convicted of the mass slaughter of thirty-two young men and boys. Married and divorced twice, he was allegedly divorced the second time because of sexual impotence. The remarkable features of Gacey's aspect structure are the ambitious alignment along the MC-IC axis disrupted by the combination irritation and ambivalence figure (irritation triangle: Mercury-Moon-Neptune); ambivalence triangle: Sun-Moon-Saturn-Neptune) *and* the tell-tale 'hole' which punctures the seventh house cusp. Mars and Uranus flank the seventh, but are outside the orb of conjunction. Holes in aspect patterns show one's Achilles heel, and where they fall in the chart pinpoints one's particular type of self-defeating pattern. The descendant weakness is its manipulative streak: planets located there are potentially aggressive and excessively dependent on an audience. Gacey's descendant cluster, Mars-Uranus-Jupiter-Saturn, speaks for itself.

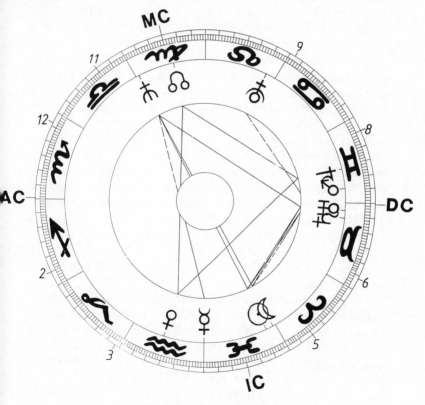

Figure 23   The horoscope chart of John Gacey.

The Sun, Moon and Saturn's sextile insulates the ego from personality conflict: Gacey probably had no idea that he was seriously disturbed. Mercury's condition is highlighted by the nerve-racking quincunx-square aspects of Uranus and Neptune. Equally important is the fact that Mercury falls at zero degree of sign and just beyond the Huber low point. Mercury at the zero degree of a sign is ill-equipped to handle Pisces' diffusion: the mind drifts aimlessly. It needs environmental protection, but in this instance can't get it. Poised just beyond the low point, Mercury experiences maximum frustration in extracting recognition from the world. Here it has neither the inner force (sign power) or the external resources (house strength) to use Uranus' and Neptune's signals comfortably. Zero-degree planets on a low point, being particularly vulnerable, are often subject to extreme overcompensation — no wonder Gacey's psychic imbalance found such an appalling expression.

Traditional astrologers will appreciate Mercury's potential mutual perception by degree. Mercury in Pisces disposes Neptune in Virgo and Jupiter in Gemini. When moved by degree, Mercury joins Mars and Uranus on the seventh or the ninth house. Jupiter is restored to its 'pillar' location on the IC, and Neptune opts for a conjunction with the Sun and Moon. Notice that Venus is also responsive to the mutual reception of Saturn and Uranus. It leaves the third for the sixth house, while Uranus and Saturn end up in the third, thereby merely restating the already prominent Mercury theme. The new Moon conjunction at the end of Pisces is particularly tricky. The Moon is separating from the Sun; it is charging ahead to an opposition with Neptune. Thus one has the desire for new starts but is muddled by Neptune and half-way sabotaged by the pull of the unconscious at the IC and the sign's wish in late Pisces to retreat into it.

The Neptune midheaven camouflaged Gacey's real instinct: he fooled the world and himself. Few of his acquaintances would have intuited that his psyche was supremely frightened and vulnerable; most, his victims included, would have responded to his seductive charm and go-getter political face that was visible in the seventh house. None would have surmised that behind the mask of benevolent leadership lurked the ingredients of such terror. The tragedy is that Gacey was probably quite oblivious to that side of his character: insulated personalities rarely recognize inner problems. Mercury's zero Pisces low point suggests that even if he had realized the magnitude of his problem, his cries for help would have been so imperceptible as to have gone unheard until it was too late. It might have helped if an astrologer had been around to hear his desperate Mercury before it gave rise to such ugly circumstances — the early recognition of deep yet undetected personality conflict is one area in which astrology can truly help.

My experience of zero degree Mercury on low points has taught me that such persons rarely feel understood by their families or friends. An element of deception is always possible in their communication, not because of any particular guile or cunning on their part but rather because of their relatively naïve, unformed sense of personal design. Words are random; communication a bit hit-and-miss. Before switching perspectives, I would like to include here a judgement made by the classical astrologer Firmicus Maternus in his *Matheseous Libri VIII*. Astrological aphorisms from the ancients are the bane of humanistic astrology; while I, too, resist the kind of astrology that infers only limited free will and which in its applied form (i.e. consultation) draws on the isolated apocrypha of the tradition, I nonetheless admit that the old material has a remarkable substance which makes it worthy of careful scrutiny. Thus for students of astrology — and not those seeking formulae that are proof positive of the pederastic instinct — I include the following (italics mine):

> Also if Venus is in the house of Mercury and Mercury is badly located, the natives are driven with monstrous desires to the bed of boys. To be exact: this occurs *when Venus is in the house of Mercury and Mercury is on the IC,* or the descendant or on the anafora of the ascendant, *or in his debility.* [5]

Firmicus Maternus' interpretation is rather seductive. However, the modern astrologer cannot in good faith equate 'Venus in house of Mercury and Mercury in the IC' with sexual perversity. Any pathology in a horoscope arises out of a combination of factors, not from just a single testament.

Mercury's sado-masochistic impulses stem less from any fundamental cruelty than from the mind's split from the body: here, it is the act of giving and receiving pain that *restores identity*. Physical relatedness, however perverse, offsets Mercury's depersonalization. Pain centres the diffused character within the body while appeasing Mercury's shame. Guilt plays no part in Mercury's sado-masochistic instincts; what does surface, however, is an undifferentiated shame which acts aggressively on the world or against the self. The culprit here is Hubris. Pride is the means by which pain-injected social embarrassment becomes *pain-preferred* social experience. Secret elitism (i.e. identification with the gods) mixed with feelings of social inferiority (i.e. ungodliness) weld the Hermes-ruled individual to pain-induced pleasure. Recall that it was Hermes' social discomfiture as a bastard among the Olympians which led him to the position of being cleverer than anyone else: he *had* to be. Though formally recognized as one of them, he behaved and was always treated as if he were of lesser consequence — something that we astrologers continue to do! Hermes thus became the Greeks' court jester, the plaything of his elders. He never acknowledged his inbuilt inadequacy nor confronted the hierarchical tyranny that held sway over him. As a result he side-saddled his way into adulthood never quite able to look straight ahead. It was his self-righteousness that held him hostage.

One case that comes to mind concerns a highly successful advertising executive whose Mercurial demeanour is marked not only by his Adonis-like appearance and scintillating way with words but also by his somewhat hostile sado-masochistic treatment of women, most of whom become vehicles for his madonna / whore fantasies. This man's behaviour, the evidence of stunted development, finds its roots in one nightmarish caning experience at Harrow. He was not from one of the old families, just a bright child from a humble background that managed to get top marks, and as a scholarship boy he never felt accepted by his peers. Although his adjustment came about through the quite deliberate acquisition of a towering intellect, this never alleviated his distress at feeling ostracized. A public beating before his superior classmates left an indelible imprint on his adult personality. Even today, despite his obvious acceptance in the world, he bears the insecurity of unexamined pride — his verbal jabs are stiff enough to kill you.

Mercury's eroticism finds expression via two other outlets: those of the trench coat exhibitionist and the Peeping Tom. Each type in their own way derives pleasure from impropriety: the one enjoys shocking passers-by, while the other achieves arousal from the secret witnessing of human nakedness. Both highlight aspects of pre-adolescent sexuality, in which 'show and tell' is accompanied by a certain level of risk. The accidental observation of adult sexual acts provides another trigger for voyeurism in later life. Dysfunction results when any of Mercury's sexual experiments becomes an end in itself. Trench coat exhibitionists are not the same thing as ordinary exhibitionists, whose essential narcissism demands genital exposure;

the former hide their insecurity behind a coat, as opposed to running naked through fountains or displaying themselves on nudist beaches. Flashers are truly ashamed of their inadequate feelings concerning the sexual relationship. But voyeurism is by no means limited to the observation of overt sexual activity; anonymity within an environment of intimacy provides another breeding ground for fantasy-related eroticism. The armchair professions, such as psychology offer a subtler kind of keyhole whereby the voyeur's prurient self-interest may be allowed to pass for therapeutic objectivity. Astrologers are similarly exposed to the temptation of deriving a kick from vicarious experience, hearing as they do of other peoples' life styles, and they must take particular care to ensure that their own sexual needs are met outside the consulting room. Yet Mercury's vigilant eye may well find a constructive use in analysis, presuming, of course, that a certain reciprocity exists between analyst and analysand. Given the vacuum that is created by time and the required intimate anonymity, Mercury's best work can take place in this environment. The French novelist, Alain Robbe-Grillet is someone who succeeds brilliantly in capturing the sexual vacuum that Mercury inhabits. His work *The Voyeur* demonstrates an emotional insularity that is characteristic of Mercurial temperaments.

> She is crying. A tear can be seen falling slowly down her cheek. The girl sits down on the bench; without putting her legs between it and the table, she turns the upper part of her body toward the latter and rests her forearms on it, hands clasped. Finally she lets her head droop forward, her face hidden in her hands. Her golden hair gleams in the lamplight. The man slowly approaches, stands behind her, stares at her for a moment, stretches out his hand, and slowly caresses the nape of her neck with his fingertips. The huge hand, the blonde head, the oil lamp, the edge of the first plate (on the right), and the left upright of the window are aligned in the same oblique plane. [6]

That Robbe-Grillet's most famous novel should be entitled *The Voyeur* is hardly surprising. Mercury observes from a veritable peephole on the 'closet' side of the ascendant, the twelfth house. The linear, somewhat disjointed, pattern accentuates an already excitable Mercury. The environmental factors focus on the somewhat flimsy structure: five planets sit on or near cusps (Venus-Saturn-Uranus-Pluto-Mercury) — is it any wonder that this author should have revolutionarized the novel's structure and the philosophical assumptions underlying it? He replaced the psychological novel with a phenomenological one known as the 'new novel', whose most revolutionary aspect was the shift it displayed in the relationship between the writer and the reader. Robbe-Grillet rejected the concept of author omniscience, the alleged privilege of speaking for a character's psyche. Instead he adopted the use of pure, linear description: human beings, actions and objects are depicted by their surface appearances, devoid of any interpretation. In offering the bare, almost skeletal facts, he leaves the reader to complete the equation: the reader-cum-author may invest passages with any reality he chooses.

While Robbe-Grillet's style suggests that his intention is objectivity, his achievement is in fact quite the reverse. The critic Victor Carrabino describes this novelist's world as 'a slice of reality, as seen and filtered, first through the eyes of the author, and second through the eyes of perceiver-narrator'.[7] Thus in the eagle-eye geometric arrangement of the passage: 'the huge hand, the blonde head, the oil lamp, the edge of the first plate (on the right), and the left upright of the window are aligned in the same oblique plane' there lies an erotic charge. Robbe-Grillet's audience may either approach or stand back, at their own discretion. This perspective of the observer to the observed is central to Robbe-Grillet's work. Mercury is used as a camera operating from its most intimate of spheres (the twelfth house), assuring a most unique and subjective one. Robbe-Grillet's loathing for the author playing God makes sense in view of his caged lion Sun with Neptune in the twelfth house on a low point and the muffled cries of his hypersensitive Moon in Gemini in the tenth house on a low point. The mainspring of Robbe-Grillet's ego is Saturn conjunct Venus on the second cusp, which accounts for the structuralist orientation. What matters is substance: in this case, the framework of the novel and its constituents. Time is another vector that is important to Robbe-Grillet. While the very reading of a Robbe-Grillet novel places the occurrence of events in the present, his works display a curious ambiguity of time and space which impose an even greater burden on the participant reader to define the novel.

Robbe-Grillet's work reveals the emotional vacuum that Mercury inhabits: it is typical of Mercury to observe humans with the same indifference it accords objects while arousing in them emotional uproar. Another of his novels, *La Jalousie* (the title is a French play on words: *jalousie* denotes both the emotion of jealousy and a Venetian blind) traces the process of a triangular relationship as seen by an unspecified onlooker (reader?) who watches the proceedings through the slats of this type of blind. Here Robbe-Grillet achieves the full scope of Mercury's erotic distance: the cerebral excesses and preference for fantasy. What is curious is how this creator's literary design, the very structure (Saturn), creates the erotic strait-jacket and how this in turn satisfies an already defined emotional isolation (Moon low point/eastern planet emphasis). Mercury's explosive opposition to Uranus across the first-seventh axis implies intellectual assault. Robbe-Grillet expressed violence by inference; he expressed passionate emotion by implication. He attacked the literary community's penchant for reductive character analysis. For him, the reader superimposed 'feeling' content in the midst of reading the novel. Robbe-Grillet would contend that rage is the product not of his carefully manipulated array of circumstances but of the reader-participant's own hand.

It is ironic, in view of Robbe-Grillet's ostensible contempt for psychology, that his works are intensely psychological; while he scrupulously avoids moralizing or speculating on the whys and wherefores of character behaviour, he nonetheless presents his characters in the process of being. This 'process' and that triggered in the reader establishes a relationship of intimacy quite unlike that produced by the earlier descriptive novel forms, but this intimacy is still contrived, still a step removed from real human connection. It is a device, a trick as it were, of an all too clever Mercury; Robbe-Grillet kids himself with respect to those virtues he holds most noble. Is it not typical of an individual to hold in high esteem those conditions which preclude the discovery of those areas that he or she fears most? Are not Robbe-Grillet's literary conventions part of a Mercurial scheme which makes the best of his own resistance to intimacy and to being pinned down?

His popularity with modern audiences comes as no great revelation: the Mercury with Uranus and its semi-sextile to Saturn states that his primary identification is with the world of objects. The abstraction of that attachment — Uranus brings about a more sophisticated disguise for materialism — is the core of structuralism. This author opts for ambiguity; we know, however, that this phenomenological bias is an effective decoy for pure subjectivity. That Mercury registers as both impotent and fertile accounts for much of its interpretive complexity. Robbe-Grillet's vision clearly displays an element of Mercurial impotence.

Let us now turn to another perspective. The image of Mercury as Priapus, a fertility god, is relatively unfamiliar to astrologers.

Few see him as a deity concerned with impregnation, still less as a passive vehicle for the life force. Yet the ancient phallic stone herms that the Greeks erected to Hermes reflect a very different Mercury, one whose seminal role lies not only in the stimulation of group growth but also in the art of taking possession. In Chapter 2, I alluded to the importance of stone monuments in the development of an acceptable system of theft: the passing traveller was expected to honour Hermes by some gift in exchange for that left by someone else. This process — the act of taking being followed by that of gratuitous getting — suggests a fertility rite. Analogous to this legend might be the act of human sexual intercourse: the assumption is that the gift will be returned in the form of a child. The secret in this instance is that Mercury effects the exchange: it is the vessel through which life might exist and one that is, quite literally, phallic. The danger here — and this is typical of Mercurial individuals — is that of overidentification with the phallus, the external vehicle of impregnation, of getting trapped in a kind of monotonous coupling at the expense of a deeper mystery.

Ibis, an Egyptian variant of Thoth/Mercury, a black-and-white feathered stork, symbolizes this deeper connection between Mercury and union. The striking feature of Ibis in contrast to the popularized white stork is its dual colouring. Moreover, the bird was known to devour serpents, yet it drank only from crystal streams. While the Egyptian stork consumed poisonous reptiles, its priests followed it to suitable water holes. Ibis ingests the diabolical (serpent knowledge) because she has access to the pure (understanding = water). By acknowledging chthonic forces — those elements hidden within the psyche — Ibis attains what the Hermeticists described as 'seven times distilled water'.

From Hermes, whose coupling resembles the stringing of beads, the Ibis aspect is very remote indeed. Too wide a difference rests between the god of the mechanical gesture and the bird of sacred ritual; the god of one-night stands just doesn't know any better. We now move on from Mercury's more sordid side to its untarnished strength: its devotion to the art of service.

Notes

1. Norman O. Brown, *Hermes the Thief: The Evolution of a Myth* (University of Wisconsin Press, 1947). See Brown's remarks concerning Hesiod's misogynistic disposition.
2. Ibid.
3. Norman Gear, *The Divine Demon: A Portrait of the Marquis*

de Sade (Frederick Muller, London, 1963). Source material for biographical details.

4. Marquis de Sade, *Justine and Other Writings,* translated from the French by Richard Seavy and Austryn Wainhouse (Grove Press, 1975).

5. Firmicus Maternus, *Ancient Astrology: Theory and Practice* 'Libri Septimus XV', translated from the Latin by Jean Bram (Noyes Press, 1975), p.248.

6. Alain Robbe-Grillet, *The Voyeur* (John Calder, 1959), p.193.

7. Victor Carrabino, *The Phenomenological Novel* (1974), p.49.

7.
Forgotten Virtue

'Blessed are the meek; for they shall inherit the earth.'
Matthew, 5:3

Mercury's forgotten virtue is that of service, usually attributed to the sign of Virgo. Warrior-cum-sage, Mercury is at once a Samaritan and a guardian angel; he is the blessed agent of whom it was written: 'I am Thoth who acquitted (or justified) the voiceless one, who protected the weak one, and stood forth in defence of his belonging.'[1] The patron of true service, Thoth encapsulates all that is Mercury in its noblest sense. He is meek and unobtrusive, yet formidable in his silent dignity: his guise of quiet modesty masks great wisdom. Thoth is both firm and yielding: 'He it is who judged the rivals and reconciled the brothers.'[2] From him we acquire truth and its close relative, love. By his actions we know his heart: he is a healer. Work of this order exacts more than altruism; it demands discipline, as well as courage. Risk taking is not Mercury's familiar mode of behaviour: experimentation is, though not within the structure of a formal commitment. But Thoth, endorses challenge. Duty and routine are second nature to him. He is able to initiate extraordinary action, and, because he exists within chaos, he may order it.

Thoth's vantage point is unique in that he is both master and servant, at once subordinate to and the equal of universal law. With him we equate the loyalty and obedience of *the master to his servant*. True disciples are grounded in a hierarchy of spiritual laws and relationships. Central to Thoth's service role is the way vertical and lateral relationships overlap; communication, while shaped by and forming part of a hierarchical model, nonetheless crosses all the established boundaries. While work is carried out within the ordered schema — mainly as a matter of efficiency or convenience — respect among servants allows lateral access (one-to-one interaction) up and down the titular hierarchy. Benefit derives from the lowliest to the highest, each contribution being valued and perceived as of equal merit.

The volunteer Thoth's main joy comes from the act of doing, of keeping busy and productive. And yet Mercury in this dignified station is often snubbed and unappreciated, even held in slight contempt — why? Take, for example, Virgo, Mercury's service correlate: one adjective that appears again and again in descriptions of this sign is 'meek'. The modern definition of this word is vaguely pejorative, anything modest, humble or lowly being regarded nowadays as self-effacing and therefore weak. Yet its original Greek meaning, 'taming or bridling of a colt', implies the harnessing of a great power, the disciplining of extremely high spirits; what has come to signify extreme docility and submissiveness was clearly once the curbing, not the destruction, of vital forces. The colt is domesticated, taught obedience, but it retains its responsiveness and freedom of movement. Mercury's service attributes also bear the stigma of a degraded femininity: that which stands back as others pass has come to be considered inferior. The notion of charity suggests feminine nurturing attributes and is thus invariably regarded as being civilized, Christian and altogether other-worldly. Because the world commands attention the forces of rationalization stand slave to the corrupt view that service is somehow the consequence of having few alternatives, whereas it is really a form of positive action and a blessing.

To the extent to which Mercury ignores its service calling, it suffers from dis-ease: efficiency breaks down, as does the alignment between work and well-being. Horoscopes with a sixth house emphasis share the same condition: unless the sixth house Mercury-Virgo person cultivates service through work, health problems intrude. The mark of the hypochondriac is the healer *manqué* who has internalized his outer duty. What, then, is Mercury as embodied in Thoth but strength in apparent weakness, power in the benign? Unlike its assailants, who would avow arrogance as opposed to humility, Thoth/Mercury gains by its veritable silence.

Mercury's volunteer spirit shines through in the horoscopes of the Samaritans and the Guardian Angels. Inspired by Chad Varah and Curtis Sliwa respectively, these organizations are the model of Mercury's good works: both show how idealism may be grounded in practical service. Mercury's influence is doubly important here because one group helps through *communication* whilst the other assists within a *transportation* system.

The Samaritans

The heart of the Samaritans' work is the telephone, Mercury's masterful invention. Its accessibility and anonymity give it a unique, Mercurial attraction for those individuals who are reluctant to seek help face to face. Chad Varah started the Samaritans in an attempt to curb suicides and over the years has achieved that objective as well as a great deal more. The key to this organization is Mercury's mainstay: communication. Its members provide a bridge or sounding board for the distressed. Here Mercury acts as guide, helper, night watchman: it is the 'third' ear of the trained listener. The unique factor in the Samaritans' work is the extent to which the Mercury principle identifies both the problem (conflict) and the solution (resolution). For those who are alone and riddled with despair, the very act of befriending evokes the healing process; the listener's just being there engages the caller's healthy impulses. Before tackling the Samaritans' horoscope, consider briefly the degree to which Mercury, in its most negative expression, is *life-avoiding*. I use the word 'avoiding' rather than 'destroying' here because Mercury need not commit suicide in order to suffer emotional or spiritual bankruptcy; it may simply hover in the vicinity of nowhere land, a necessary consequence of self-imposed redundancy.

Suicide is the zero-sum game, the ultimate guarantee of having the last word and for some, that is a first. Because suicide is a form of communication, albeit one-way, this type of behaviour is essentially Mercurial. However complex the motivation for committing suicide may be, the act itself sends out the contradictory messages of anger, helplessness, vengeance and retaliation. Suicidal persons share Hermes' marked ambivalence in relation to the world. Life as it is is disappointing, without purpose. Those who do kill themselves are effectively saying: 'Life as it exists is not worth living; death is a palatable alternative.' The individual in question sees no way out of the predicament, and suicide becomes the lesser of two evils, the forced alternative. The paradox is that depressed people tend to commit suicide when they have begun to feel better. Their decision coincides with a momentary burst of optimism which convinces them that death will do the trick. Whereas previously the individual was immobilized by pain, now he or she becomes anxious to do away with that pain once and for all.

The suicidal person reveals other Mercurial traits apart from that of holding a negative world-view: namely, dichotomous thinking, a limited emotional range and social inhibition. Black and white thinking is Thoth's curse when it imposes too many 'shoulds' and results in cognitive shutdown. The mind's ability to process alternatives — to see its way clear — becomes impeded. What happens then is that the individual opts out of the bewildering conditions of blanket condemnation (Thoth's trick) and ambiguous moral licence (Hermes' trick) by causing his or her mind to go blank. On the emotional front, Mercury taken to extremes is equally impoverished: the mind rationalizes or discounts 'feeling' values, those emotions that are present seeming vaguely fraudulent. The overall impression is one of feelings being manufactured *as if* they were authentically present, reduced to the level of sadness, gladness or madness, with no overlap or subtlety. Social inhibition is not, on the face of it, Mercurial, yet it should be recalled that one of Mercury's major hang-ups is commitment to a relationship; although Mercury is able to partake of multiple liaisons, these are frequently shallow and unstable.

The midnight hour was chosen because it marks the official beginning of a day. I prefer midnight charts to noon charts because they seemingly capture the 'root' of the matter. I also use the midnight hour when doing corporation charts. Although I wrote to Chad Varah about the precise time of the Samaritans' first call (the date is given as November 2, 1953 and the place as London), he never replied. A volunteer later asked him for that information directly. Varah recalled my letter but flatly refused to divulge any information about the Samaritans other than that already published.[3] He gave no reason for his refusal, so I was left to speculate as to whether it was a matter of policy or of prejudice against astrology — not inconceivable, in the light of his clerical background.

The triangular shaping of the Samaritans' horoscope gives dynamism: three-sided patterns allow Mercury the elbow it needs to experiment. Purpose functions within the force of a Mars-Jupiter-node dominant triangle. Expansion is not only rapid, intentional and international, but central to the organization's well-being. The sheer scale of the Samaritans' activity (one million calls or visits per annum) attests to the power of Mars-Jupiter. Mars-Jupiter squares are notoriously energetic as well as profligate; placed within the larger pattern, excesses are reduced. Despite the broad objectives held by the Samaritans, the incomplete aspect structure (Uranus-

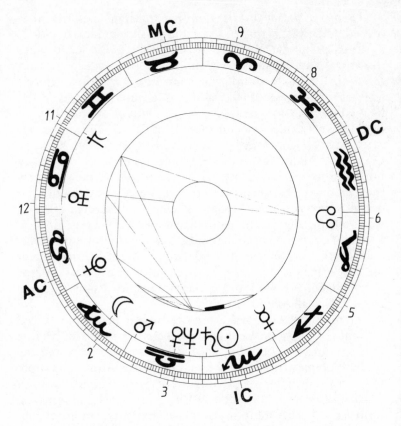

Figure 24   The horoscope chart for the Samaritans.

node-Neptune-Saturn) implies that lacunae exist somewhere.
Broken cardinal T-squares desire efficiency but are unable to sustain
it. Rules may be constantly in a state of flux and therefore a source
of annoyance to the community. The need for the setting up of
new centres may take precedence over administrative perfection.
Notice how Saturn and Neptune make a 'hole' in the aspect pattern,
both forming part of the same unhinged T-square; Saturn-Mars'
faint semi-sextile cannot offset the thrust of this T-square. Holes
are like punctured tyres: the atrophy of energy they cause may be
so gradual that the actual collapse comes as something of a shock.
They also share Mercury's elusive character; Mercury appears
indefatigable, yet abruptly something blows from sheer exhaustion.

The presence of a hole in this map warns the volunteers of their tendency to overidentify with their role as Samaritans. The inefficient use of time, an over-tolerance towards the manipulative client and an inability to transfer responsibility to other volunteers could well be symptomatic of an impending flat tyre.

Little ear arrangements (Saturn-Mars-Mercury) are easily overlooked when they appear within large, complex structures, but this is a mistake. Tiny aspect configurations often identify the essence of the individual. Little ears or 'eyes' are natural antennae: they suss out all that is obvious and also not so obvious in a situation. For this reason the Samaritans' little ear is especially appropriate — what more effective structure is there for the art of active listening? No other network hears innuendos quite so accurately. Mercury's location inside the little ear accentuates the role *awareness* plays for the Samaritans: the process is firmly attuned to subliminal communication. Mars' presence speeds up the mental and physical reflexes, while Saturn anchors the organization's sensitivity as far as judgement and common sense are concerned.

The Samaritans' third structure (Jupiter-Pluto-Neptune, equalling specialized talent) confirms the broad-scale altruism. Talent resides within the realm of the cognitive (Jupiter), perspective (Pluto) and love (Neptune). The aspect structure defines the *modus vivendi*: the way one lives. When clear and unobstructed, Mercury's game plan is straightforward, but when that pattern is haphazard, the cues become a shade garbled. Mercury must then rely on the ego planets for more specific instructions. The ego planets show Mercury's habitual slant, whether physical, emotional or mental; they indicate how it presents the self to the world. Strong ego planets buoy up Mercury's confidence. The posture and the manner of speech reflect this self-assuredness, and the personality conveys an attitude of having a 'divine right' to be here. Weak egos communicate the reverse. Confidence is diminished, as is the belief in one's justification for living, the personality shows itself as cowering and tentative, if not apologetic. The Samaritans' ego profile shows that none of the ego planets are strong. The Sun hangs by a thread to Saturn and makes no other aspects. The intelligence is absorbed in the excesses of the sign (Scorpio, concerned with issues related to life and death) and in the demands made upon it by the environment. It relies on Saturn's control mechanism for security. What better astrological equivalent is there for a group whose central objective is altruistic and whose collective ego echoes the low self-esteem of those it serves? Suicide prevention counts on the Sun's pull towards life. The Samaritans' Sun's tentative link to Saturn reflects the ambivalence present among the suicidal; the spirit is grasping for a *raison d'être*.

What, then, of Mercury? To which planet does it owe allegiance here, and how does its intrinsic duality fare against the estranged Sun-Saturn? None of the ego planets show inordinate power, Saturn having a slight advantage of influence because it rests within a complete aspect pattern. Saturn-ruled Mercury has carefully defined skills grafted onto Mercury's anonymous, friendly manner; it also confers a sharp, accurate ear and a great deal of common sense. However open the Samaritans may be to the material that is presented to them in confidence by callers, they nevertheless move within tightly controlled spheres. This is fortunate in the light of the aspect structure's leak and the ego planets' relative lethargy.

The Samaritans affirm life by acknowledging the autonomy of the individual, and in so doing they reverse any negative imprints that may have been made by the father (the Sun) and the mother (Saturn). By presuming this autonomy — in effect, by drawing together the elements that go to make up the nurturing, affirming self — they validate the significance of the caller in question. The organization is unique among suicide prevention groups in its policy of non-intervention: its members do not chase would-be suicides, neither do they trace telephone calls. In resisting the paternalistic rescue impulse, Samaritans not only dignify human choice but assure freedom by giving responsibility, not removing it. Allowing people the prerogative to choose life over death engages the will — the only source that is forceful enough to sustain life. Mercury is thus a psychopomp, an escort of souls. Although Saturn guards Mercury's vagrant passage, entry into the Samaritans' expansive world-view lies via the Sun in Scorpio. Thus it is at the portals of impasse and in utter darkness that Mercury's real work begins. The confrontation and acceptance of the spiritual abyss of the soul's separation from God invokes the power of healing. But how does Mercury effect this change?

We know Mercury to have the benefit of logic and patience (sextile to Mars and semi-sextile to Saturn). Alert and accurate, it makes an excellent listener. Notice, too, that here Mercury is stationary retrograde at zero degree of Sagittarius; it has in effect just entered Sagittarius and is turning back into Scorpio. One senses the exhilaration and optimism of having left the emotional struggles of Scorpio, the relief at having escaped from such intensity, *and yet* the awareness of an obligation to venture back underground.

The stationary position implies waiting, whereas Sagittarius constitutes hope. The mood here is that of reflection, of a pulling back from impulsive action as characterized by Sagittarius. This Mercury placement calls to mind Siddhartha's lesson of thinking and waiting.[4] Calling the Samaritans is at once an act of chance, of faith, that maybe just this once help will arrive, that one might not need to kill oneself after all, or that the irretrievable act might be postponed.

The implication of Mercury situated at the zero degree is that lessons unlearnt the first time around, especially those concerned with mental or emotional balance, must be faced again. The retrogression brings deliberation in all such matters, something that is quite unfamiliar to early Sagittarius. Planets at zero degree appear strongest because they in fact are at their most primitive. The fiery impulsiveness of Mercury-Sagittarius, representing the instinct for escape, is rightly curbed and told to think again — or to at least wait. Chad Varah's own Mercury also sits between 29° Scorpio and zero Sagittarius. This degree area seemingly describes a preoccupation with living and dying, with the nature of giving up or going on. Mercury in retrograde against Sagittarius and in mutual reception with Jupiter would explain why Varah prohibited his volunteer co-workers from testifying to membership of a particular religion.

The Guardian Angels

The Guardian Angels patrol New York City's twenty-four-hour transportation octopus, the subway system. Lords of the tubes, the Angels work unarmed alongside the NYC Metropolitan Police. Initially distrusted by the city authorities, suspecting they might be self-appointed vigilantes, the Angels now hold its official sanction.[5] It is to their credit that cities both throughout America and abroad have called on them to introduce similar programmes in their areas. The Guardian Angels' main job is as divine protector: like Hermes, they prowl the highways in search of bandits, thieves and other ill-mannered beings. Their work is essentially on-site deterrence. Quick and alert, the Angels share Hermes' acute sensitivity to change in the environment; they know when danger lurks. Their very presence on the trains comforts passengers obliged to travel by subway after dark.

The Guardian Angels' clear orientation toward service is hard to miss in this horoscope dominated by planets on the western horizon and a strong Virgo-Aquarius emphasis. Their chart shows

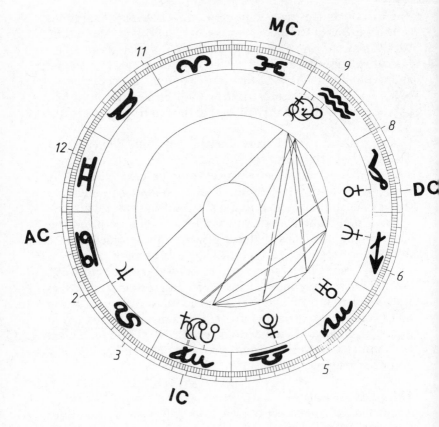

Figure 25   The horoscope chart of the Guardian Angels.

a need for public contact but within clearly defined circumstances. The vertical aspects indicate a need to differentiate themselves from others. The lack of oppositions, despite the Venus seventh cusp placement, denotes their uncompromising but polite stance towards aggression. The squares from Sun-Mars to Uranus and Neptune to the node act as a buffer zone between the Angels and the populace of the subway. The squares mirror the Angels' natural defences: physical fitness and the force of numbers. The Guardian Angels work by silent intimidation — the prolonged stare. Unarmed policing takes the form of hyper-vigilance and an aura of fearlessness as symbolized by their familiar red berets. The four-sided structure accompanied by a linear form marks a group driven by security but willing to take risks to get it: the Angels clearly prefer a cosy, insular existence but are adept at shifting from that state into the realm of unpredictable street fracas. Security is both a private and public objective. Within the organization one notes an obvious 'family' network and a sense of belonging.

Volunteer organizations endure because of right motivation and effective leadership. The prospect of volunteers patrolling New York subways with a view to curbing crime is in itself daunting; but to take on the additional task of training street people who *might have just as easily been the menace* previously or in the future, is truly courageous. Curtis Sliwa did just that — but how? Sliwa taught the volunteers not only specific skills, such as the martial arts, but also personal discipline. He gave them a new-found dignity and a sense of social responsibility, stressing the importance of duty and of group respect. Above all, Sliwa exhibited the drive and initiative needed to do it; he demonstrated the virtue of action over words. Sliwa's system works because it cultivates Mercury's finest habits: it relies on duty and humility. Accountability to oneself and one's peers is a major factor in the Angels' success story. This is particularly evident in the method it uses for the selection of volunteers. Angels may propose new volunteers, but only under penalty of personal liability; should an Angel recommend someone who is later rejected for breaking the rules, the proposer is automatically barred from service. The Angels run a tight ship: they have to, otherwise their own privilege of membership is dissolved.

Service organizations ostensibly render service; and yet few actually do so. The reasons for this vary, but the main ones are a lack of clear objectives, faulty leadership and an ill-conceived approach to the fulfilment of tasks. What gives one volunteer group sufficient clout to run long after other groups have quit? For the astrologer the main theme is the aspect structure, and weak structures simply do not last. Mercury's task is that of defining and implementing duty. The backdrop against which it is constantly tested is that of group/individual ego strength. The Guardian Angels' horoscope reveals that the Sun, Moon and Saturn are all strong. The Sun is awarded a slight preference because of its elevation, its location after the ninth cusp and the number of its aspects. Notice that Saturn and the Moon are situated quite prominently in eleven degrees of Virgo, that area which according to Huber understanding represents maximum sign power. Mercury is thus influenced by the high-mindedness of the Sun (Aquarius, ninth house placement) with back up from Saturn and the Moon, anchored respectably at the base of the chart. The group's identity is thus grounded in practical skills as well as in an altruistic purpose.

Mercury plays an especially important role in the Angels' map because it is the most elevated planet, sits in the sign of alleged exaltation (Aquarius), is located on invert point (the area of perfect temperance as far as planetary activity is concerned), and is the final dispositor of the chart. The conjunction to the Sun reinforces Mercury's single-minded attitude. Notice, too, its mutual reception with Saturn, which emphasizes the care that Mercury takes when it comes to such matters as judgement, discipline and timing. An outstanding feature of this chart is the number of planets (the Moon, Venus, Saturn, the Sun, Mars and Jupiter) on or near cusps. The presence of a large number of cuspal planets always brings the group or individual concerned to the foreground. The activity of such planets is visible, distinctive and in some cases out of control; for this reason it is necessary to check the overall structure for signs of stability as well as indications of Mercury's capacity to reason before taking action. Were Mercury out of control in a chart too moved by environmental cues, one would not expect stability to be possible. Recall that the Angels work in unusually dangerous circumstances and must therefore have some degree of chutzpah (cuspal) in the charts, balanced by the more seasoned judgement of planets found towards the middle of the houses. What better situation than to have the planet of common sense perched on the invert position of restrained, yet measured behaviour, as it is here?

Notes

1. Patrick Boylan, *Thoth, Hermes of Egypt: A study of Some Aspects of Theological Thought in Ancient Egypt* (Oxford University Press, 1922) p.36. Thoth epithets abound in this volume.
2. *Ibid.*, p.38.
3. Chad Varah, *Samaritans in the Seventies* (Constable, 1977). An account of the Samaritans' history. I also drew on my own first-hand knowledge of suicide prevention volunteer networks.
4. Hermann Hesse, *Siddhartha* (Peter Owen, 1954) p.65.
5. Information obtained from Guardian Angels' publicity material, plus a direct interview with Lisa Evers, co-leader of the Guardian Angels, in 1980.

8.
Lord of the Roads

'Seek out some city that is young. The secret is to make a
city, not to rest in it. When you have found one, drink
in the illusion that she too is eternal'[1]

Mercury flourishes in the big city, whose high-speed momentum
and promise of variety it treasures. It appreciates the transient,
unsettled character of urban living because it perceives change as
an opportunity, not as a threat. This type of existence approximates
to Mercury's impersonal, offhand manner. Like Mercury, city-
dwellers are streetwise. Their pace is fast, upbeat, yet strangely
mechanical — particularly during the rush hour. The acid test for
urban sensibility is the extent to which one elects for anonymity.
Mercury chooses quite happily to be anonymous: it is neither
resident nor stranger, but a face among the many addicted to
strap-hanging and newsprint. Mercury demands mobility, and the
city obliges.

The people-watcher Mercury delights in metropolitan areas where
train stations and park benches abound — the native voyeur can't
get enough of the city's sidewalk circus. Obviously, not everyone
who inhabits a city is Mercury's ally, for not everyone chooses to
be there; only those who openly adore that hectic jumble qualify
for the title. Practical experience with individuals in three major
cities, New York, London and Paris, as well as in small towns whose
populations are 5,000 or less has shown me that those who *prefer*
the bustling metropolis to a more leisurely rural tempo are uniquely
Mercurial. This may be because enthusiastic urbanites share
Mercury's allegience to polarity. Research by the German sociologist
Bahrdt points out that urban atmospheres are polarized between
'decided freedom and unconsciously observed limitations or

controls'[2] — what better description could there be for Mercury's intrinsic duality? Bahdt shows that the more rural the environment, the less prenounced is the condition of polarization: could this mean that the more active the planet Mercury is in the horoscope, the more inclined an individual would be to experience conflict and thus enjoy cities? Could this also imply that the less vigorous the Mercury spirit, the less likely a person would be to cherish conflict and urban settings? I believe it does.

Urban terrain caters to experimental life styles; it allows Mercury's erotic side *carte blanche*. Given that planet's affinity with sophisticated communities, 'big city' horoscopes ought to include a rather distinctive Mercury. Take London, for instance. The British

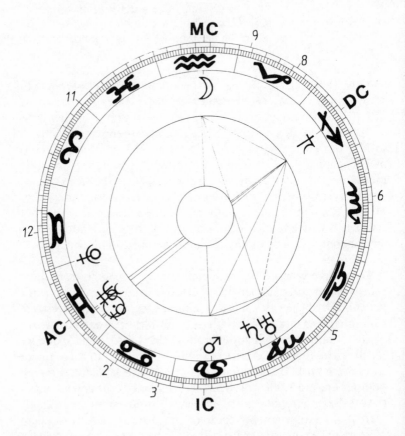

Figure 26   The horoscope chart of London.

capital is a paradox: an international market-place and centre of world trade (Mercury-Jupiter themes) but at the same time a cluster of tiny villages unique unto themselves. London is both urban and suburban: for those who live in its centre, it is a state of mind — not at all frantic, and whimsical, if not poetic. Its pace may be faster than that of Cornwall but is still quite unlike the whirlwind of sister cities New York and Paris. Yet all the characteristics of the urban milieu are in evidence: a transient population, high-level commercial enterprise and a multitude of cultural blessings. Most claim that London society is a closed one, frightfully snobbish and inpenetrable; the fact is that this city does exclude a certain quality of arrogance, but one that is easily displaced by the Lisa Doolittle treatment — in other words, learn to speak properly!

London's horoscope shows a city that is both aloof (meridian emphasis) and accessible (horizon emphasis). Stability is a priority but not always possible (broken patterns). The chart contains several unaspected planets, including Saturn and Pluto, and incomplete aspect structures. What is particularly striking is the incomplete, mutable T-square which marks a desire for efficiency but a difficulty in achieving it. The transportation services are notoriously unreliable. The Moon's MC position in opposition to Mars accounts for the air of lofty self-possession that Londoners exude. Meridian planets create barriers between the resident locals and visiting foreigners. Thus, those travellers (as represented by Jupiter in Sagittarius in the seventh) who ironically adore London, find themselves quite often ostracized by the meridian axis' iron curtain. The welcome wagon runs on one criterion: literacy. Entry into the Londoner's world falls along the horizon axis, populated, appropriately, by Mercury-Jupiter. Mercury plays an inordinate role in London's chart: not only does it dispose of six planets, but is also rises in conjunction with Sun, Venus and Neptune. Mercury's power stands out also because all the neutral planets (Mercury, Jupiter, the Moon and Neptune) tenant angular cusps. This makes it hypersensitive to incoming and outgoing signals.

The planets around the AC endow it with a standoffish intensely private demeanour which is often misconstrued as snobbishness but is really the product of extreme self-consciousness. The Gemini strength here places communication at a premium, but communication of a particular order: speech (Mercury) is the determining factor up and down the social scale. In some circles, having the same accent erodes blocks, while in others evidence of similar education helps. Humour in all instances is one ploy that

Gemini accepts. London's Gemini cluster might be understood in terms of 'inside jokes'. Acceptance within this sphere demands a knowledge of the context or 'inside story' on which wit turns. For those who know the basis of this in-house humour the experience of London can be a highly intimate one, but for outsiders unaccustomed to speaking London's language the contact can mean an icy dressing-down, be it in pub or philatelic society.

Let us now consider the map of San Francisco, urban mecca of the West Coast of the United States. Unlike Los Angeles, its bumbling neighbour and rival, 'Frisco' exudes a big city atmosphere: it is a sophisticated, well-educated city known for its taste and refinement. Mercury's presence is unmistakable here, making itself felt not only in the renowned San Franciscan intellectual community but also in the city's open toleration of unconventional sexual behaviour. San Francisco is the recognized seat of sexual liberation, particularly where the Gay Rights Movement is concerned. Mercury derives added pleasure from the fact that it is an active commercial centre and a busy seaport.

This horoscope has the vertical eastern bias that is typical of staunch independents, and the absence of oppositions suggests that its people are uncompromising social pioneers. The eleventh house Aries planets show an elitist perspective and a particular arrogance towards outsiders. (This characteristic is shared by New York City!) Despite the cultural finesse, at heart San Francisco remains crude and free-thinking — a maverick. Mercury conjunct to the Sun, Uranus and Pluto assures it a modern outlook and reformist instincts: its citizens can't help but speak out abruptly and persuasively, particularly with regard to social values. Mercury's backdrop (Moon-Neptune-Venus) is decidely aesthetic, but the Mars-Jupiter-Saturn link injects life into an otherwise lazy, sluggish streak brought about by the prominence of the first three planets: it was, after all, San Francisco that invented the slogan 'Make love, not war.' The trendy, ever-popular rising Gemini moon keeps the place at least one step ahead of the times, making it not merely fashionable but a pace-setter creating new fads and popular theories. This city anticipates the moods of an era to come: it is an urban weathervane. The streets of San Francisco are the source of ideas to be disseminated some five years hence.

To write about cities without mentioning that gauge of all things urban, New York City, would be to cheat at the exercise. Penfield's horoscope for the Manhattan transfer (a few trinkets for an island) is box-shaped: by this account, New York is incredibly stable. Four-

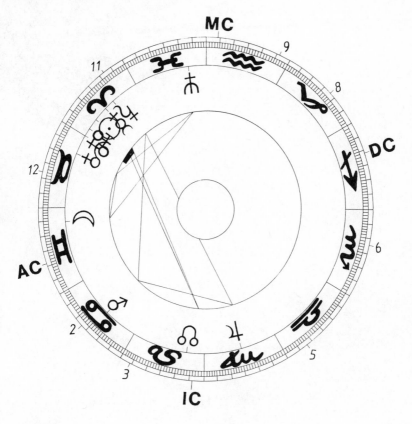

Figure 27   The horoscope chart of San Franciso.

sided horoscopes mean the amassing of substance: could one even begin to question New York's clout in terms of finance and power? The Taurean stellium around the eleventh house focuses on the city's abject materialism: nowhere is the pitch of commercial excitement quite so evident as in this the financial capital of the world. Mercury in Gemini, translated, conveys the city's outlook: 'Money talks.' New York is the sybarite's paradise, and its concrete jungle is Mercury's own particular brand of nirvana. However crowded or rat-infested the city might be, its heart, Manhattan adodpts an 'island mentality', being both worldly and provincial at the same time. It is an escapist's workshop and a dilettante's delight, containing literally anything that one could want — at a price.

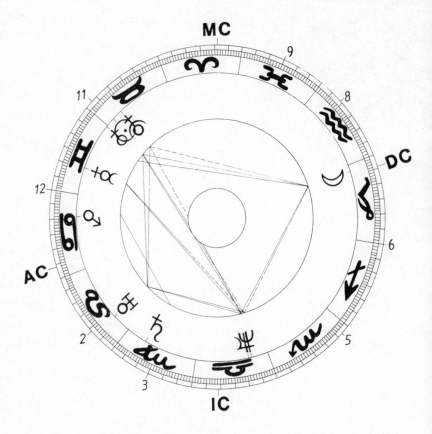

Figure 28   The horoscope chart of New York City.

Mercury's cul-de-sac location shows New Yorkers to be innate voyeurs and closet know-alls. They sit on the outside looking in, posing now and then as experts on everything. Poseurs in every field find rapid camaraderie in New York's 'as if' society, where even illusion is okay provided it's an original. New Yorkers are also snobs. To the real New Yorker, anywhere outside Manhattan is a cultural backwater; and yet the bulk of its inhabitants moved there from the boroughs. Mercury, with its liking for expediency, helps transplants to quickly forget whatever origins they once had.

New Yorkers are also street people: they live *en route* to somewhere else. Commuter chaos is routine, yet everyone affects the condition of hurry and invariable arrives late. Fortunately for them, and for those obliged to wait, New York is likewise the newspaper centre — the proliferation of newsprint is such that anyone stuck in a subway is bound to find suitable reading material for killing time! Word magic has its blessings. Mercury trine Jupiter Neptune is liquid gold for a city attuned to advertising and publishing. The same flowing Mercury aspect gives New York its special optimism when a crisis forms. Transportation strikes, electrical black-outs, crime increase, bankruptcy — this city has known them all. Yet the spirit of urban living (a kind of philosophical chuckle) is that hanging in there counts and staying flexible is critical. The Manhattan horoscope tells us that nothing could really rock the community sideways — except, perhaps, the

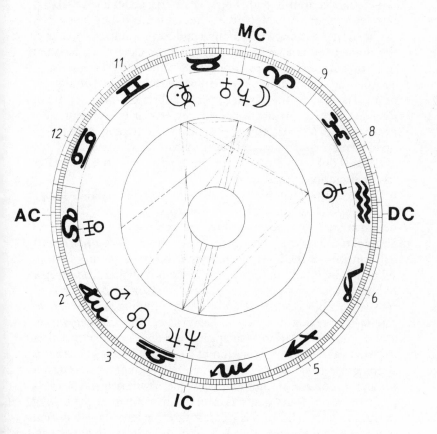

Figure 29   The horoscope chart of NYC Stock Exchange.

New York Stock Exchange, Mercury's ideological twin. For the merchant god Mercury, trading is his livelihood. The city is the market-place, the seat of his activities. The connection is a close one, for the two are near-namesakes: Hermes' Roman title and the word *market* come from the same Latin base, *merces*.

The New York Stock Exchange has a horoscope with an ambitious, risk-taking structure. The oppositions along the MC-IC axis affirm growth potential, while the three-sided figure shows the Stock Exchange's mutability. This is in direct contrast to New York City's map, which shows it to be acquisitive rather than distributive in function. The Stock Exchange's dominant aspect pattern involves Mercury-Jupiter-Pluto, which indicates large-scale transactions concerning other people's assets, generally carried out by telephone or telex. Mercury's agitated Pluto square tells us the market is an insomniac: even though trade occurs during set periods, the market reacts to influences around the clock. The Mercury quincunx Jupiter promises surprise: the rumour that such-an-such a corporation is about to merge with so-and-so may create a ripple or a tidal wave in the market index. Subtle or abrupt shifts of direction are in the nature of quincunxes, especially to Mercury. We turn now from Mercury's more general urban and commercial make-up to its more practical significance in business matters. As Wilde said, 'It is only by not paying our bills that one can hope to live in the memory of the commercial classes.' [5]

Business astrology differs fundamentally from natal astrology in one respect: companies lack the free will that individual human beings possess. For this reason business horoscopes work more like Skinner rats than the horoscopes of individuals. A company chart will function at the level of the lowest common denominator of astrological symbolism: for example, if Mars is blighted in the sense of having too few aspects, the sales momentum and initiative of company employees are not likely to be astounding. The astrologer cannot assume that corporations have a moral sense; leaders within a particular corporation may apply their own personal moral or spiritual values to the formation of a company ethic, but that is a separate matter. And from the material point of view, unless it has ample tools and ammunition available, a company will be likely to attain only marginal gains. (Dealing with companies that belong in this category calls for the greatest possible tact!) Ammunition in the astrological sense, means a solid foundation. In particular, this requires a powerful aspect structure backed up by appropriate significators related to the organization's purpose. Unless their maps have a cohesive structure, businesses are likely to flounder: rickety astrological frameworks mean that they rarely withstand the pressures of difficult progressions or transits occurring during the first few years of operation. The company with an unstable map is at the mercy of internal leadership difficulties. Its management may yet stop the ship from sinking, provided, of course, that the individual manager's horoscope dynamics allow this to happen.

Mercury's role within business or corporate set-ups is identical to that in natal charts. Here its main responsibility is as the agent for company objectives: it handles all routine transactions, support services and distribution functions. It is also the company's mouthpiece, generating all its inside and outside publicity. Mercury's task is made all the more simple if company goals are clear-cut. Ideally, the product should be firmly etched in the chart symbolism: for example, a cosmetics firm ought to have a prominent Venus or Libra, an electronics firm an emphasized Uranus and an agricultural group the beneficial presence of Virgo. Successful ventures need a mixture of endurance (Mars-Saturn), efficiency (T-squares) and financial savvy (Moon-Venus-Pluto). There must be room for growth (Sun-Jupiter) and evidence of imagination (Neptune). An all-round winner usually includes a dose of traditional luck, such as Venus-Jupiter combinations. While Mercury is *the* commercial planet, too much of it at the expense of other features is counterproductive. This would be the equivalent of having too many Indians and too few chiefs. The next two horoscopes illustrate Mercury's positive involvement in outstanding achievement and its distracting quality where mediocre accomplishment is concerned.

Corporation X is a family-owned agricultural holding company designed primarily to offset personal tax liabilities. The business is an honest but inefficient one. Assets are few; the profit margin almost nil. Since its foundation it has made no appreciable gains through its own efforts. Currently X is absorbing assets from another family-run citrus operation because of an inheritance. X's main themes are continuity and convenience; there is no sign of an expansionist policy or of a desire to change circumstances. Corporation X's disjointed aspect pattern broadcasts the fact that its focus is probably weak. Vitality diminishes, as does ambition, under these conditions — this is no hot contender for a business boom! The broken structures here (Mercury-Uranus, Sun-Venus, Venus-Jupiter-Moon) indicate mismanagement, poor planning and bad judgement. The hole (the space between Venus and Uranus)

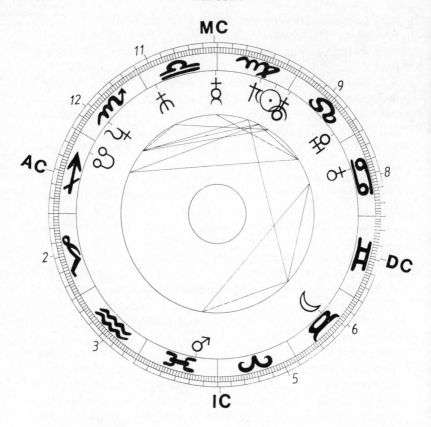

Figure 30   The horoscope of Corporation X.

in the eighth house implies both a drain on revenue and a degree
of indebtedness; this particular pattern does not augur well in terms
of corporate purpose. The eighth house is the tax house, and Venus
and Uranus jeopardize the firm's chances of peace in this area: any
loophole X might wish to make use of may be denied it by the
Internal Revenue. Another clue that Corporation X stands on shaky
ground is the topheavy planetary focus above the horizon-making
horizontal aspects — something I equate with shuffling papers from
one side of the desk to the other. There is a reluctance to look more
closely at the deeper rationale for the firm's existence. While it
is definitely an above-board operation, it is decidedly naïve when
it comes to hidden motivation: Jupiter does reach into the lower

sphere, but it is isolated from the other planets.

Mercury's importance, while exaggerated, is no real help. The midheaven conjunction means that the sibling-run corporation is steeped in number-crunching and procedural razzmatazz. Mercury on the MC is the veritable court reporter: everything is taken down verbatim, making the records — of what little has transpired — superb. Mercury's zero-degree Libra position highlights the vulnerability and indecision that characterize X: peace-keeping between siblings and spouses accounts for much of the firm's day-to-day activity. Mercury's sextile to Uranus reveals X's particular weakness: technology. The company thrives on equipment, gadgetry, supplies, etc. Too much time is devoted to the purchasing

Figure 31   The horoscope chart of Corporation Y.

of new materials and too little to the actual business of orange-growing and profit-making. The overall picture is too fragmented for outstanding success; yet despite its flaws, X has endured. The Moon-Taurus pre-cusp sixth house shows the firm's crisis temperament and instinct for survival. If it weren't for the abundance of earth in this chart, Corporation X would have probably discontinued operations. As things stand presently, X may dissolve into a mere name. Its long-standing manager wants to go on social security — and he hasn't bothered to train anyone else to take his place.

Corporation Y is quite another story: it embodies all those things precious to corporate gold. The aspect structure is a substantial one, planets and aspects occupying a good proportion of space around the wheel. Efficiency is highlighted, as is company productivity. Y is an electronics firm whose reputation and success are well documented. The electronics planets (Sun-Mercury-Uranus) occur within an efficiency figure, thus showing maximum possibility for attaining stated objectives. Initiative is high, due to the cardinal influence, and staying power is indicated by the Moon-Mars-Saturn ties. Y's exceptional growth dramatized by the Mercury-Jupiter-Neptune arrangement, is doubly emphasized, thanks to degree strength: Mercury and Jupiter both sit on the degree 'bonus' area, eleven degrees, thirty-two minutes of any sign being the jackpot. This testifies to Y's extreme potential for commercial success; the combination of inherent talent and pure know-how that are evident in the structure cannot lose. These things, united with the Taurus Moon endurance/money instincts and the blessing of Venus-Jupiter make life at the British firm of Racal very exciting indeed. This concludes our walkabout with Mercury. We have seen Mercury in a number of disguises and sundry roles. Turn now to a more detailed investigation of Mercury interpretation: the 'how to' section.

Notes

1. Thornton Wilder, *The Cabala Book V: Dusk of Gods* (Albert & Charles Boni, Inc., New York, 1926, p.229).
2. W. F. Heinemeyer, *The Urban Core as a Centre of Attraction* p.86
3. Ibid.
4. Dieter Prokop, 'Image and Functions of the City' in *Urban Core and Inner City* (Proceedings of the International Study Week, Amsterdam, 1968). Leiden, E. J. Brill.

5. Oscar Wilde, *Phrases and Philosophies for the Use of the Young* (Printed for private circulation, p.5).

9.
Interpreting Mercury

'The very best map reader has to suffer some shocks
when he comes face to face with reality'

Josephine Tey[1]

In order to judge Mercury with any degree of finesse, the astrologer
requires a priori knowledge of the *context* in which it functions.
Context here refers to the precise psychological and environmental
factors that shape its activity. The reason this is crucial is that no
other planet is so uniformly moulded by its surrounding influences.
The Moon, while equally receptive, is not at all obliged to act on
the world; it can choose to avoid contact (although inclination would
favour it) and simply reflect the conditions around it. Mercury,
by contrast, *must*. As messenger of the ego, Mercury's life is rarely
his own: he must attempt some interaction with the personality
and the world. To discover Mercury is to unravel the meaning of
the entire horoscope. Barraged by contradictions, astrologers
typically either give up on Mercury altogether or limit their
interpretation of it to such remarks as: 'Mercury in Taurus equals
the practical thinker' or, slightly more inspired, 'A materialist with
a husky voice.' This is patent nonsense; such observations, though
they might be quite literally true, still constitute a gross
underestimation of the influence of a planet that spins its web over
the whole psyche.

Deciphering its significance can be a weighty task unless carried
out systematically. The first step entails evaluating the chart with
two questions in mind. Number one is: Does the horoscope support
healthy communication patterns? (Meaning: Does Mercury have
sufficient access to all parts or corners of the personality?) Number
two is: Does the environment provide outlets for Mercury's
communication? (Meaning: Once the personality has organized

messages for the outside world, does the universe pay attention?) In order to answer these questions we might begin by enlisting the principles taught by the Huber method of chart delineation. For the sake of brevity I have modified certain of the Hubers' points and added a few of my own. [2] There are five, namely: hemisphere distribution, aspect structure, ego bias, gender bias and environmental bias.

Hemisphere Distribution

The horoscope is divided by two axes: the meridian and the horizon. These axes further separate the map into four divisions: north, south, east and west. Each of these sectors represents a particular way of viewing the self in relationship to the universe. The horizon axis, known also as the ascendant-descendant line, describes the self in relationship to others; while the meridian axis or midheaven-*Imeum Coeli* path depicts the self in a state of separation from others. As emissary of the ego, Mercury incorporates various attitudes arising from both these axes.

Horoscopes showing a strong alignment across the ascendant-descendant axis adopt egalitarian views of relationship: contact is sustained at the 'I-thou' level. Charts picking up the meridian's plane accept hierarchical views of relationship, the tendency here being to perceive the differences, rather than the similarities, between people. These distinctions are drawn at the level of social position and standing, the emphasis here being on individual growth rather than on conscious merging with the crowd.

Mercury *shares* information in the horizontal maps, and its hidden assumptions are based on the notion expressed by 'I, meaning we, the people'. In vertical charts, Mercury *gives* information; messages from this group imply the somewhat patronizing attitude: 'I, meaning we, the *cognoscenti,* the élite.' Horizontal maps capture the flavour of folk singers, their information being passed along informally from one generation to the next just as the moods and traditions of an era are continued through the music. Vertical horoscopes, on the other hand, share the principles of formal architecture: the information they convey is built on certain laws or foundations and then becomes individualized as it passes through the eyes of the individual architect. Creative principles operate from both axes, but the purposes differ. The ascendant-descendant line challenge requires involvement, human exchange; the midheaven line demands separation and independent recognition. A disproportionate stress

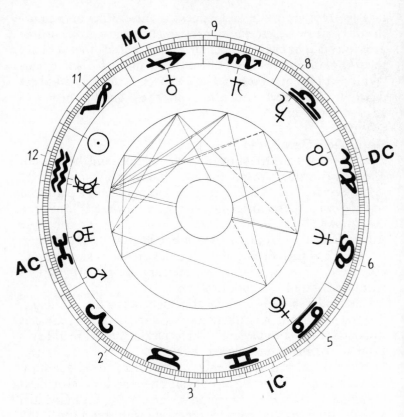

Figure 32 Chart A, vertical focus, coherent structure.

on either axis can spell trouble. An exaggerated concern for the opinions and affairs of others provokes dependency and a lack of individual profile: one's image melds with that of the collective. Such persons lose their autonomy, their capacity to think for themselves. Likewise, top-heavy arrangements along the meridian can preclude growth in the area of human relationships: the need to be 'different' overshadows the instinct for co-operation. An exaggerated emphasis, particularly at the midheaven, can denote a dictatorial streak. Alienation, whether from the self (horizon stressed) or from others (meridian stressed), is hardly conducive to a balanced unfolding of the personality. The hemispheric subdivisions offer further details of the nature of Mercury's governing terrain:

South	Objective thought. Goal orientation. An impersonal attitude. Individual achievement. A focus on the future.
North	Subjective thought. Experience orientation. A personal attitude. A focus on the past.
East	An obligation to the self. Introversion. A focus on the present.
West	An obligation to others. Extroversion. A focus on the present.

Mercury's actual position within a particular sector is not that important. Far more relevant is the distribution of planets within sectors that contradict each other in terms of purpose.

Table 8   Mercury's activity in the four sections of the chart.

Chart B illustrates an extremely difficult combination. There are two groupings of planets — one in the eleventh / twelfth house and the other situated in the seventh: there arises a conflict between the need for public recognition and that for personal withdrawal. This chart is further complicated by the fact that the signs tenanting each house are also alien to their surroundings. Notice Leo, an extremely extroverted sign, situated in the most impersonal introverted corner (the twelfth house) and Pisces, the most introverted sign, located in the most accessible introverted house (the seventh). Because planets are found there one knows immediately that Mercury will need to work overtime in an effort to accommodate two categorically opposed attitudes: that task is carried out by the aspect structure. The next step, therefore, is to look at the ways in which the planetary aspects support Mercury.

Aspect Structure
The aspect structure and its relative coherence denotes the central organizing feature in the horoscope; it provides the key to the personality's motivation and its capacity to fulfil objectives. The aspect structure also gives an appreciable insight into the relative capacity of individuals to withstand stress. These factors become particularly pertinent to an understanding of Mercury as they gauge firstly the degree to which action follows idea and secondly the extent to which the stress load either stabilizes or inflames Mercury's nervous disposition. Coherence and aspect strength in a chart show vitality, stamina and volition. A brief general survey of charts drawn

Figure 33   Chart B, horizontal focus, diffused structure.

according to Huber specifications permits the astrologer to judge
the subject's propensity for stability or instability. Tightly woven
mosaics bestow far more confidence and a far higher degree of
personal autonomy than open-ended ones. The latter structure
(dominated by wide aspects/dotted lines) signals a restless,
impressionable personality with few natural tools for integration,
although *this may of course be learnt*. Loose aspect patterns
capitalize on Mercury's already diffuse nature, and for this reason
require careful examination when it comes to estimating that
planet's degree of efficiency. Chart A shows an unusually strong
aspect structure: motivation is high, as is the ability to cope. The
planets form tight aspects both vertically and laterally, indicating
the probability of a high level of personality integration. Chart
B, on the other hand, characterizes the weak aspect structure: the
character depicted is elastic and impressionable, lacking initiative.
Chart A is that of a highly accomplished woman whose

organizational savvy and managerial skills make her a first rate volunteer executive. Her abilities continue to grow, stretch and be pruned; the second, that of an accomplished bridge player whose 'genius' level IQ does not sit well within the scatter pattern. Because B is unable to handle ordinary pressures (although tournaments do not seem to bother him), he is usually classified as the gross underachiever; the fact is, as the horoscope shows us, that growth will only come from *learnt* self-determination within the confines of a pressure-free milieu. While A's potential arguably matched or was less than that of B, the tools of A's trade made her access to her innate talent that much simpler.

The overall aspect structure may be classified as linear, three-sided, four-sided and mix. Briefly, each of these categories corresponds to an attitude or world-view. It is from this structure that Mercury draws its main thrust for interpreting action.

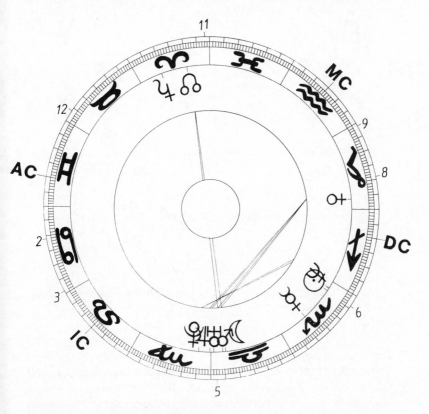

Figure 34 The Linear Arrangement.

Linear arrangements

These are the most typically Mercurial, as they belong to subjects who dart about from one interest to another at lightning speed. Such persons are highly mental, erratic and indifferent to such issues as security and the lack of it. The 'outsider' perspective of the linear personality is apt to earn the person in question the tag 'unstable'.

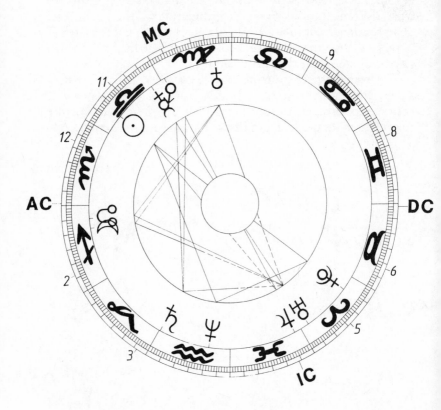

Figure 35 The horoscope chart of Friedrich Nietzsche, showing three-sided aspect structures.

Three-sided aspect figures

These support Mercury's desire to know and to be inspired as well as to daydream. The subject's spirit of adventure overrides any sense of the mundane. Such persons are known to be dynamic, continually changing, but they can also adopt a lazy, non-committal streak.

Four-sided aspect structures
These appeal to Mercury's practical side. The emphasis lies on the
creation of a stable environment, the status quo taking precedence
over innovation. Material goals haunt this kind of chart.

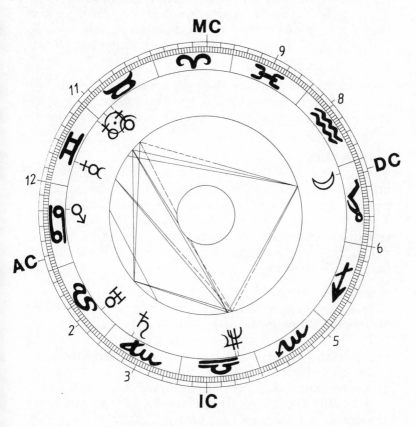

Figure 36   The horoscope chart of New York City, showing four-sided
aspect structures.

Aspect Types
If it is the graphic appearance which identifies the personality's
driving force, then it is the combinations of aspects which signal
its *modus operandi,* the way the individual concerned functions
in the world. Aspects fall into three groups: Type A,
action/motivators (conjunctions, opposition and squares); Type
B, talent/pacifiers (trines, sextiles); and Type C, consciousness
raisers (semi-sextile, quincunxes). These types may occur either alone

or in combination with one another.

Single aspect horoscopes

These are quite rare. The governing aspect type, whether A, B or C, dominates the character. Motivation is ordered by action, repose or fantasy. Such individuals exhibit a marked incapacitation in some field of life experience. Mercury's condition is uniquely important here as it signals the ways in which balance might be restored.

Double aspect horoscopes

These are the most common. The temperament is dual: it vacillates back and forth between one mode of action and its opposite. Here Mercury's natural dualism feeds the person's tendency to see the world from an 'all or nothing' perspective.

Triple aspect horoscopes

These are the maps with the greatest potential for growth: here action is tempered by thought and inspired by natural talent. This type of personality has the best chance of stability and individuation. Stress is manageable, relaxation available and consciousness accessible. Three-category aspect horoscopes are not free of disequilibrium; their inner structure merely ensures that any imbalance is short-lived.

Combination of double aspects[3]

Type AB shows a marked ambivalence regarding his or her working philosophy. The prototype AB is both a workaholic and an escapist and is usually unaware of the underlying conflict. Motivated by contradictory impulses, the AB individual seeks tangible success in the material world as well as a stress-free, cushioned existence. Continued mismanagement of energy resources generally results in ill-health. The AB personality subjects itself to continuous pressure during the week and then lets all hell loose on the weekends. Heavy social drinkers and drug abusers occupy this category. So do sports fanatics and television addicts. Mercury's task in the predominantly AB horoscope is to build insight and perspective. While Mercury may actually reinforce AB's tendency to compartmentalize experience, Mercury may also be enlisted to recognize that propensity and thereby lessen the extreme see-saw disposition of *Type AB*.

Type BC individuals coast through life rather than struggle. Their *modus operandi* is thought, inspiration and imagination. BC dispositions flourish in the theoretical or academic climates. The level of procrastination is high, the output low. Mobilizing resources can be difficult. Armchair philosophers, members of this group gain by having energetic partners whose adrenalin levels suffice for two. A followers rather than a leader, the BC person is easily manipulated by those with authoritarian temperaments. Mercury's lessons of analysis and discrimination ground idealism. Physical exercise vitalizes the otherwise sleepy disposition.

Type AC mixtures thrive under stress: The pattern denotes a hyperactive, frenzied nature. This combination oozes creativity and is usually ambitious although often ill-equipped to realize its goals. Renowned for having a touchy, artistic temperament, AC personalities specialize in rash, impulsive decisions. They are short on planning, patience and foresight. Mercury can lend some reason to AC's inspired furore; however, more often than not, Mercury exacerbates AC's natural irrationality. AC shares AB's inclination towards ill-health. Mercury's physical agility and traditional association with the breath makes it an ideal ally when it comes to the yoga instruction AC needs. AC people really must slow down lest they should burn out prematurely. (Unlike BC, this type never goes on vacation!)

Huber Assessment of Ego Strength[4]
Below is a modified version of the Huber method of measuring planetary strength. (There are, of course, other ways of assessing planetary strength. Readers are encouraged to try this in conjunction with others such as astro-dynes, cosmodynes, ruler of the nativity, etc.) Two points should be noted first of all: firstly, the astrologer must use KOCH houses for Huber evaluation, and secondly, the orb schedule attached must be used for determining the condition of being aspected or unaspected. Wide aspects are designated in chart examples by dotted lines.

Hemispheres
The ego planets (Sun, Moon and Saturn) prefer to be located in these horoscope areas.

> Sun: Elevated in Houses 8, 9, 10 11
> Moon: Horizon in Houses 12, 1, 6, 7
> Saturn: Base in Houses 2, 3, 4, 5

Degrees
11°32′ represents the maximum intensity of a sign's quality. Planets at 0-29° of sign are at the minimal expression level of that sign.

House Position

The Hubers have determined that within each house structure there exists three areas of particular importance: that of maximum visibility (cusp), that of maximum efficiency or effectiveness (inverse point) and that of minimum visibility and efficiency (low point). If ego planets are situated in one of these three positions, this suggests a level of relative environmental strength. Low point falls roughly two-thirds of the way in from the cusp. The invert point is approximately one-third of the distance from the cusp.

Number and Quality of Aspects

Aspects are divided into three groups:

(i)   Conjunctions, squares, oppositions
(ii) Trines and sextiles
(iii) Semi-sextiles and quincunxes

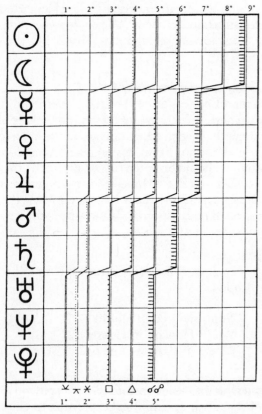

Figure 37   Huber's orb schedule.

The higher the number of aspects, the greater the strength of the Sun, the Moon and Saturn. Ideally, all three categories of aspect types will be included in a strong ego planet arrangement. In some instances, none of the ego planets are particularly powerful. In this case, the Hubers recommend development of the ascendant and north node signs.

Ego Bias

Ego bias, as defined by the relationship between the Sun, the Moon and Saturn, shows the degree to which Mercury's function of communication is either aided or hindered by the personality. Robust egos are natural communicators, whilst fragile ones find expression more difficult. As one's self-esteem colours one's capacity to act on the world, the astrologer's role is to find out just how strong the ego in question is and to facilitate ways of integrating it. Aspects between the ego planets describe one's sense of purpose and feeling of belonging. The Sun, the Moon and Saturn not only infer the level of personal autonomy but also the *subjective* experience of family. Specifically, Sun-Moon represents the father-child relationship, Sun-Saturn the father-mother relationship and Moon-Saturn the mother-child bond. By extension these combinations manifest in Sun-Moon (one's capacity to act creatively and independently), Sun-Saturn (one's attitude towards formal obligations and responsibilities such as marriage) and Moon-Saturn (one's innate capacity to accept and give nurturing).

An absence of contact between the Sun, the Moon and Saturn indicates a rejection of family models. If the aspect structure lacks coherence, this can postpone maturity. The reasons for protracted adolescence are numerous; generally, however, the person's home background and early conditioning had little relevance to his or her make-up; such individuals are often dubbed the 'black sheep' of the family. Related problems include an initial difficulty with authority figures, a reluctance to defer gratification and inappropriate choices when it comes to forming relationships. Here the individual may attempt to define himself or herself through a father — or mother — figure, but this attempt invariably ends in disappointment. When the Sun, the Moon and Saturn form no tie, the self-image is hazy, due to unhelpful role models. Children lacking aspect among the ego planets need special educational guidance. However, if Mercury is well aspected in this kind of chart, it will spur on the talented underachiever whose undisciplined way generates such havoc in the classroom. On the other hand, the child with no aspect between the ego planets plus a poorly connected Mercury will be likely to withdraw from group activity and require help in self-assertion. A disconnected Sun, Moon and Saturn are mitigated by a powerful aspect structure. The advantage of this set-up is that the individual, though a late developer, will bring to the world something unique. The resistance to being moulded in the traditional fashion of their heritage and milieu results in a quite highly developed individuality.

All three ego bodies joined shows the strong ego, but not necessarily the happy or healthy one. The keynote here is an aura of confidence and self-assurance that is often lacking in the group just described. These people are usually mature for their age, although not necessarily precocious. Their jauntiness and high degree of self-regard irritate their peers, especially during adolescence. A strong Mercury guarantees few problems as far as vocational planning is concerned. This trio mixed with powerful verbal skills may show an insensitive, no-nonsense practical mind, dubbed the overachiever. If Mercury is not well placed, the ego speaks authoritatively on subjects about which it knows little; the personality can be smug. Ego planets knotted together promise early successes, although such achievement often lacks originality. The reason is that when the ego is totally insulated from the world, it feels disinclined to pursue new avenues of thinking.

Ego Planet Mentor for Mercury

Mercury's awareness is further refined by the specific potency of the Sun, the Moon and Saturn. One of the three ego planets acts as arch-mentor for Mercury's communication habits. Occasionally, all three ego planets are strong, in which case Mercury is almost certainly exceptionally able. Alternatively, in charts where none of the ego planets shine Mercury relies more heavily on cues supplied either by the aspect structure or the environment. Three ego planets well placed obviously magnifies chart potential, whereas three ego planets obscurely positioned suggests that the individual will have to struggle to realize his or her expectations.

The Sun, as the strongest ego planet, inclines Mercury towards a thinking model. If Mercury shows dominant traits, leadership as well as creative and/or theoretical abilities probably ensue. A weakly configured Mercury with a solar bias will still need to be in charge, but its effectiveness will be diminished.

The Moon lends Mercury a feeling motif. The emphasis is on relationship, on contact with others. Energetic Mercuries pursue teaching, public relations, etc., the urge being towards compassionate communication. This Mercury intuits more than it thinks but is able to stand back from its own observations. Mercury in weak profile implies that the interaction/contact theme continues but at the expense of objectivity: the mode of thought and behaviour becomes habitual, unconscious and compliant. Writers appreciate a lunar force backing Mercury as it gives them the skill to capture atmosphere and nuance.

Saturn at the helm means that Mercury's horizon is physical: the focus moves from a thinking or feeling model to an applied, practical one. What counts for Saturn is application, not theory. Here communication thrives on facts and details; precision and efficiency are the bywords. Saturn-controlled Mercury is the bottom-line mentality: either something works, makes money, or it doesn't. Body consciousness is increased, as is physical agility. Timing is impeccable and judgement sharp — these are the time and motion experts. Mercury emphasized deepens the affinity with the physical sciences; it augments the need to consume knowledge. The influence of Saturn aids the memory. These individuals are repositories of information: walking encyclopedias. Mercury weak means that the subject benefits from clear-cut, systematic teaching, and here Saturn's disciplinary thread helps provide the necessary focus.

Ego Defences

One way in which the psyche handles conflict and danger is by adopting defence mechanisms. These may operate in a positive, adaptive way or in a negative, self-limiting, 'defensive' way. As agent of the ego, Mercury devises various schemes for protecting self-esteem. The type of defence that is made relates to Mercury's primary influence, whether the Sun, the Moon or Saturn.

Sun
The threatened solar temperament hides behind elaborate intellectual ruses. Pride splits ideas from the emotions connected with them. The Sun rationalizes its mistakes; it finds plausible reasons for its faulty behaviour — a defence strategy that is also common to BC aspects. Yet such rationalization, when used positively, allows the bruised psyche room and the means to get back on its feet; it gives objectivity, a detachment from experience that would otherwise be painful. Provided this approach does not

dominate the person's entire behaviour, it constitutes a healthy adaptation to the routine psychic injuries that plague living.

Moon
Lunar defences reside in the realm of projection. Here sensitivity gives rise to the exaggerated and erroneous belief that it is other people, not the subject, who act objectionably. AC aspects share this tendency to attribute the disagreeable in themselves to others. However, the positive side of the Moon's adaptability lies in its capacity to identify and emphathize with others' emotional vulnerability.

Saturn
Saturn's defence tactic involves denial and repression: it erects barriers between the self and reality. The deliberate elimination of unpleasant facts may well be appropriate in the case of uniquely stressful conditions (such as concentration camps), where it enables the psyche to survive. The blocking out of trauma suffered in childhood is another example: such repression may be necessary for a certain period, until that time arrives when the individual feels able to confront his or her past. Healthy denial and repression occurs in the form of sublimation, whereby the person consciously decides to avoid certain forms of thought and/or behaviour in favour of others. To give one example, the discipline of the ascetic entails a repression of the physical impulses, but this denial, being consciously chosen, does not haunt him or her in the way it might others.

Gender Bias
Mercury is bisexual. It is capable of reflecting both masculine and feminine consciousness. Yet both males and females resist its feminine component. Western culture is to blame for the lop-sided view of it as the logos-laden archetype. There are no Western myths which ascribe Mercury to the female sex. Nor is it my view that there should be. Mercury is properly seen as an adolescent man-child in the *process of becoming* fully conscious. The fact that Mercury rarely does achieve full use of the masculine and feminine principle is immaterial. For our purposes, Mercury's very struggle to reconcile its outer physiological maturity (masculine) with its inner psychological immaturity (feminine) is the source of much difficulty for both men and women. Admittedly, this is changing.

Mercury is in transition: males are reluctantly tapping feminine values, whereas females are actively suppressing them in the interest of worldly success. In the West, it is men who have the distinct advantage, as their socialized self, which is rational, corresponds to Mercury's valued half. The Mercury-emphasized Western woman is at odds with her socialized femininity, which is relationship-orientated, not ideas-focused; this female identification with a masculine consciousness sabotages her own feminine consciousness and inadvertently reinforces the prevailing ethos.

The strength of an individual's Mercury merely asserts the fact that issues related to consciousness will be relevant to a person's individual growth. The astrologer must judge each Mercury separately.

Given that Mercury is currently undergoing a process of transition, certain behavioural cues that emerge at this time can help the astrologer to assess the state of its development within the personality of the individual whose chart is under consideration. Take, for instance, the case of a strongly Mercurial female. Such an individual will be attempting to deny the hold that the feminine principle exerts over her personality by virtue of her gender; thus when she becomes involved in any exercise of a strictly logical nature she will unconsciously bring into play emotional factors which really have no place in it. What she may consider to be her voice of authority will actually have the stridence of a foghorn. Militancy and passion, in a man or a woman, imply a corresponding imbalance in Mercury's feminine side. The way that this planet can short-change the feminine point of view shows itself differently in a man's horoscope: here, an intrusion by Mercury's feminine aspect into the conscious mind results in a kind of atmospheric poisoning. The man's normally straightforward, deliberate style of communication degenerates into a sarcastic, often evasive, whinge.

Sign Degree

According to the Hubers' work, signs find their maximum expression at 11°32′. Planets located within the range of 9-14° may be judged strong from the sign perspective: that is, from their innate capacity to express the sign's quality. Thus Jupiter at 11°32′ Capricorn exemplifies the best of Capricorn: its organizational sense, its practicality, long-range planning, etc. Planets located at this degree have such pronounced characteristics that 'instant', guess astrology will frequently home in on that sign rather than on the Sun, Moon and ascendant. Planets at 0-29° of sign are problematic. The zero-degree planets are often misread as powerful because they are so noisy. In reality, this noise is like that of a new-born baby:

planets in early degrees represent a primitive level of expression, as yet undeveloped. The attributes of the sign will be visible, but its power and reliability remain to be acquired. Alternatively, those at the end of the sign (28-29°), represent energies that are on the wane, in state of deterioration. Both these categories carry an anxious, nervous quality which jeopardizes the fruitful expression of the sign. Planets located in the strong zone still need the support of aspects (energy movers) and the environment. Without them, the intrinsic power of the sign may simply sit there, unobserved — in effect, wasted.

Signs and Houses

According to the Hubers, the signs govern inherit predisposition, while the houses refer to environmental conditioning. Sign quality denotes the natural resources possessed at birth. This may be observed quantitatively by degree (0°0′-29°59′) or understood qualitatively, in accordance with the meaning of the zodiacal sign. Houses are the 'impress', the external circumstances which mould and shape early behaviour. While signs relate to innate conditions, houses identify learnt responses. The maturing process consists of the organism's struggle to achieve some form of balance between self-determination and instinctual desire on the one hand and outside expectations, the dictates of the environment, on the other. The sign-dominated personality resists all manner of training offered by the world, his or her behaviour is ruled by instinct and a desire for self-preservation. The house-ordered personality exists for the benefit of the world: in other words, for someone else. This type of disposition tends to function at maximum distance from its own private wishes and perspective. When either characteristic occurs in the extreme, the sign-ruled soul may be judged primitive and the house-ruled one an automaton.

While the Hubers use sophisticated measures to evaluate the exact relationship between the individual's abilities and his or her environmental support, our interest is to see how these factors affect Mercury. The reason this planet comes to the forefront yet again is that it negotiates the deal between signs and houses. If, for example, the bulk of planets are evenly distributed throughout the cardinal, fixed and mutable houses (and cardinal, fixed, mutable positions within houses), it may be inferred that the environment allows a reasonable opportunity for the work of the initiating, completing and distributing functions: Mercury will thus have the support system it needs for fulfilling multiple tasks.

CARDINAL HOUSES (1, 4, 7 and 10)

Cardinal signs   Environmental opportunity plus the talent needed in order to initiate action. There are the dangers of hasty action and a low level of determination when it comes to carrying out plans and completing projects.

Fixed signs   Environmental opportunity for growth coupled with an instinct for stabilizing and consolidating values.

Mutable signs   Environmental opportunity to make changes in circumstances, plus the desire to do so frequently. A tendency to disperse their energies.

FIXED HOUSES (2, 5, 8 and 11)

Cardinal signs   Stable environment checks impulsive action. A desire to attain long-range stability.

Fixed signs   An unchanging milieu accords with the drive for security. A danger of stalemate and inhibited growth.

Mutable signs   Environmental conditioning limits the expansion of thought and ideas. The possibility of acute frustration.

MUTABLE HOUSES (3, 6, 9 and 12)

Cardinal signs   A free-floating environment meets the individual's instinct for action and change. The level of excitability is high; the stability of place and/or action is low. Restless, impulsive thinking.

Fixed signs   Loosely woven environmental structures clash with the inner instinct for stability. An attempt to pinpoint, to hold down what is elusive, felt to be futile.

Mutable signs   The environment and the instincts combine to the extent that both seek change for change's sake. The possibility that ideas or actions may remain dormant, unformed due to a heavy emphasis on thought rather than on action or stability.

Table 9   The influence of Mercury in the signs and houses.

Having discovered Mercury's universe, our next step will be to consider its potential dominance and its innate characteristics, efficiency and flexibility. While our preliminary work may help us to appraise Mercury's relative strength, other important factors now claim our attention.

Dominance

Rarely does Mercury assume a primary significance in the horoscope, mainly because it is always modified first by its reigning mentor (Sun-Moon-Saturn) and second by any precise aspects that it makes. Mercury's angularity does, however, assure it high visibility. House cusps, being doorways, allow Mercury ease of access to the world. Mercury placed near the first, fourth, seventh and tenth cusps, and, to lesser extent, the intermediate cusps guarantees that communication rules the personality. The individual's physical appearance, style of movement and so on will be decidedly youthful, nervous and highly strung. Their speech is quick, and their written style is often telegrammatic. Their life's vocation is usually one that incorporates an instinct for verbalizing, such as teaching, journalism, telecommunications and transportation — anything which maintains mobility is okay by Mercury's standards.

Close aspects to Mercury heighten the need for and the quality of the expression, the precision of the aspect being the prime consideration when it comes to detecting the form that this planet's activity will habitually take. Exact aspects focus Mercury, whereas loose aspects distract it. These statements apart, partile aspects (0°0' orb) certainly appear problematic, though it is hard to say why. The analogy drawn earlier between Mercury and the nervous system might shed some light on the matter. Partile aspects imply that no gap (orb) exists between sensor and receptor: the freedom to connect is missing. This area of the horoscope corresponds to the mysterious transformation or charge that occurs when two bodies interact; it also approximates to a tiny release valve whereby extreme tension is slightly reduced. If this space is lacking, Mercury's situation is similar to that of a socket receiving so much excess voltage that it burns out (the theme of the Cazimi, page 54); the planet aspecting Mercury thus welds its point of view onto Mercury's consciousness and there is an absence of freedom. It would seem, therefore, that for clarity of interpretation one needs precise aspects but ideally those which are just outside the hundred per cent partile. Weak aspects confer too great a gap between sender and receiver. Messages thus transmitted will be vague, inconsistent; their inefficacy might be compared to that of someone who begins to speak and whose voice gradually tapers off to nothing, even though the lips are seen to be moving. Dominance by both position and aspect to Mercury is best shown by the chart of that model communications wizard, Alexander Graham Bell.

Bell's horoscope reveals a horizontal direction, identifying

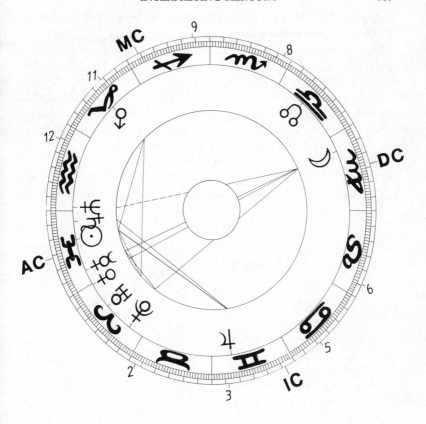

Figure 38   The horoscope chart of Alexander Graham Bell.

service / contact as a focal part of his life. The eastern focus along the horizon shows that while Bell devoted his life to the role of a teacher of music and speech to the deaf, he never lost sight of his individuality. He was described by family members as being both aloof and eminently approachable. All three aspect categories, A, B and C, are present, indicating high learning potential. Mercury's location on the ascendant in very close opposition and in a tight semi-sextile to Pluto shows that communication will be extremely important to him. The Moon's association with the public and Pluto's tie to the masses suggest that communication will have large-scale implications. This is further substantiated by Jupiter's midheaven rulership and position in Gemini, near the third cusp.

Type AC Mercury aspects to the Moon and Pluto confirm Bell's restless creativity; Mercury's angularity hints at his preference for teaching the deaf by means that are oral rather than manual. While the Sun, the Moon and Saturn are technically out of orb by conjunction or opposition, their proximity to the angles overshadows the vulnerability of ego. Both the Sun and the Moon possess strength, validating the levels of intelligence and sensitivity. Thus it is hardly surprising that Bell should have offered mankind its most useful Mercurial tool, the telephone.

Weak Mercury near angles frustrates or delays communication; the need to express oneself remains paramount but the process of interaction is seriously undermined. This may take the form of non-

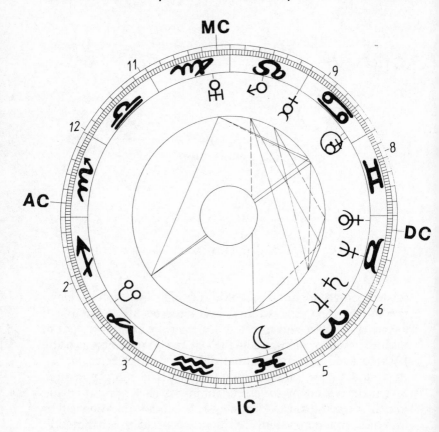

Figure 39   The horoscope chart of Helen Keller.

stop talking which irritates and annoys one's audience or a serious impediment to speech or communication. A strong Sun showing will and intelligence plus a healthy Saturn for discipline can offset this deficiency. Helen Keller's chart illustrates this point admirably.

Helen Keller is reported to have made the statement: 'Life is an exciting business and most exciting when lived for others.'[5] The salient feature of her chart is the emphasis of planets in the Western hemisphere, denoting considerable extroversion and dependency on others. All three aspect categories present give maximum learning potential. Mercury's position near the ninth cusp augments the need to externalize ideas. Loose aspects to Saturn and Pluto disclose flaws in the signals used for transmission. The fact that the Sun, the Moon and Saturn are disconnected slows character development but increases the likelihood of originality and exceptional maturity. The Sun's elevation and aspects lend power to Mercury in the guise of leadership qualities and intelligence. Saturn in the shadow of Mercury's sixth house (meaning the fifth house side of the cusp) puts the accent on discipline, endurance and the need to overcome physical crises; its rulership of the third house and weak square to Mercury again show early learning problems. Thanks to the patience of teacher, Barbara Sullivan, Helen mastered reading by touch and eventually conquered speech. Mercury's ninth house position won her world-wide respect as a lecturer and author: her books have been translated in over fifty languages. The fixity of Mercury in Leo surely helped her in this massive undertaking. Interestingly, Bell and Keller remained friends throughout their lives: note the complementary hemispheric positions. Bell's chart is essentially Eastern or connected to the self, while Keller's is the exact opposite, revealing her deep devotion to others and to her teacher in particular.

A good example of Mercury's emissary capacity is seen in the chart of the United Nations. Negotiations by the UN to end the 1982 conflict in the Falkland Islands proved completely unsuccessful — a look at the strength of Mercury in the chart below will reveal why.

An obvious characteristic of the UN's chart is the emphasis on the north-west quadrant. The attitude is subjective and very much attuned to the idea of satisfying an image as well as to that of pleasing as many people as possible. The orientation is slightly tilted, showing a certain need to differentiate itself from the collective impulses of the various participating nations. While this is, clearly a linear formation, none of the aspects form a coherent network;

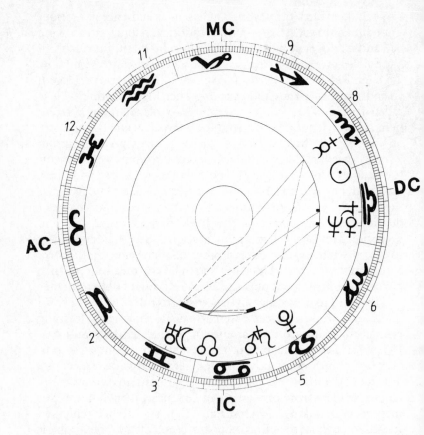

Figure 40 The horoscope chart of United Nations.

the energy is dispersed, ineffectively mobilized. Three types of aspects are present, which indicates maximum learning potential; however, the loosely woven structure weakens the motivation. The prominence of Type AC aspects, together with the linear pattern, shows a naturally Mercurial disposition. The activity around the UN is decidedly Mercurial, but the question remains: is it effective? Mercury's seventh house proximity to the Sun promotes public expression. The squares and quincux to Pluto and Uranus exacerbate Mercury's sensitivity. In a natal chart these would overload the nervous system, resulting in frequent and chronic agitation or insomnia. Mercury's position in Scorpio forming a square to Pluto lends an air of authority to group expression, but it needs the service of a benevolent ego.

The UN's Sun, Moon and Saturn form practically no aspects. None of the ego planets are particularly well favoured, either by sign or house, which means that Mercury's role is an isolated one. The aspect structure minimizes stability. The ego remains dormant, with a corresponding tendency to over-react. Mercury's elevation and angular house placement assure the UN recognition as an institution invested in communication. However, the weak Saturn, void in earth, and the Moon's excessive mutability whittle away at efficiency: a great deal of talking and paper-pushing goes on, but with very little impact.

Efficiency
The efficient Mercury is an industrious one. Productivity arises from variations on the following combinations:

1. Cardinal/fixed T-square and grand square are inherently practical. Mercury's inclusion in one enhances the probability of competence.
2. Mercury-Saturn contacts: Saturn's natural efficiency tones down Mercury's wayward disposition. This may occur *with or without* a direct aspect from Saturn to Mercury. Saturn's prominence by aspect, house or degree can override any need for specific connection.
3. Mercury sextiles: Sextiles add method, continuity and precision.
4. Prominent Virgo, Capricorn, Taurus or Saturn's other sign Aquarius. Mercury need not tenant these signs to acquire their virtues: earthy efficiency spills over into Mercury's consciousness.
5. Mercury's location after the cusp up to the Huber Invert point (roughly one-third distance). Mercury approaching a cusp (the shadow area) is easily inefficient: the anxiety and restlessness of precuspal positions wastes energy.
6. A controlled Moon: the habits and emotional disposition correlate with efficiency, therefore the Moon's stability is crucial. The mind may exhibit an unusual orderliness because of Mercury-Saturn, but a heavy lunar overlay, especially to Uranus and Neptune, can override this effect. Moon-Uranus temperaments invent their own rhythms, which rarely jell with those present, while Moon-Neptune types may have no system whatsoever. Assuming that Mercury is strong, Moon-afflicted personalities master routine best within their own closely defined sphere (private logic and sense of order is welcome at home, but not in your average civil service office).

Mercury placements in earth signs specify efficiency along certain themes: Virgo holds the record for clichés on tidiness, yet is not at all uniformly fastidious in thought or action unless the Moon is placed there. What is evident with Mercury-Virgo is that it sees detail, appreciates sequence and can order tasks appropriately with a minimum of fuss. The advantage this combination has over others is that it gets things right the first time, partly out of natural perfectionism, partly out of just knowing to dot i's and so on — a Virgo emphasis is crucial for a copy editor.

Taurus's star quality is common sense. Efficiency stems from what might be construed as a negative virtue: its inherent acquisitiveness and reluctance to part with matter. Any work that undermines the objective of gain is struck off the agenda. Mercury-Taurus's matter-of-fact, albeit obstinate attitude promotes businesslike conduct.

The most efficient of the earth signs is Capricorn. The forming of objectives stimulates productivity; it also encourages enterprise and expediency. Natural clock-watchers, Mercury-Capricorn arrives on time and notices whether others did or not. Office-memo masters and superb managers, members of this group quickly earn the title of 'efficiency expert'. Ambition plus a taste of Machiavelli's view that the ends justify the means give Capricorn top marks in productivity (Machiavelli had Mercury in Gemini but Capricorn rising).

Contraindications

Lethal to businesslike efficiency is the quincunx: individuals loaded down with several avoid order. Unless these souls populate a creative freelance environment, the chances are their presence will be short-lived. Quincunxes put elephants on telegraph poles and confuse company chiefs with window polish. There is no conformity here, no sense of protocol: priorities get mixed up. No filing system ever deserved Mercury quincunx clerks. Documents and letters end up misplaced: Mr McDschota finds himself under 'Cabbage Products'. Secretaries of this ilk never last, and as cooks come and cooks go, this cook went — and quickly! Other deterrents to smooth operational functioning are wide aspects, a preponderance of fire signs in the horoscope and too much Gemini. Sloppy orbs make for sloppy thinking: the energy scattes as it is never entirely focused. Overdoses of Mercury's first sign, Gemini, lower concentration. Pluto can help here in terms of tightening the attention span, but it has its own predicament of being mildly paranoiac. Activity never has any straightforward significance; there is always some reason behind it. Looking over your shoulder for traces of evidence that others are watching is unlikely to generate much forward motion. Pluto may bring a cloak-and-dagger efficiency to work carried out in the analyst's chair and at Scotland Yard, but it is not much help to the average white-collar worker. Mercury-Pluto's subversive refusal to take direct routes to anywhere backfires in the realm of ordinary paperwork where two plus two must be four. For the Plutonian the natural response is: 'Who said? How come? Why not 2 + 2 = 7?'

The fire signs Aries and Sagittarius are very quick to act but notoriously lax in cleaning up the mess left behind. Efficiency drops, not because of dithering but rather because of all the errors committed in split-second decisions. Characteristically, Sagittarius-

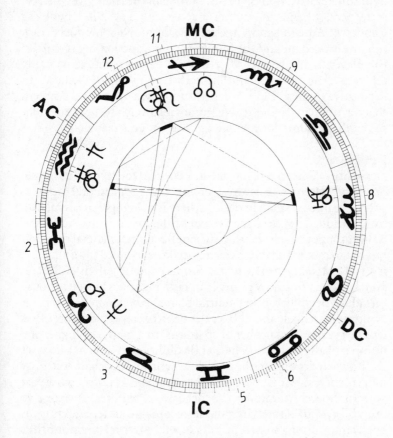

Figure 41   The horoscope chart of Tycho Brahe.

or Aries-Mercury finds details taboo, a tendency that surfaces equally often when Mars and Jupiter are out of control. Leo, however, manages to be efficient, probably because of its natural fixity.

Tycho Brahe's central contribution to 16th century astronomy was his tireless and patient recordings of planetary bodies. Brahe's precise observations aided Kepler in his discovery of the Laws of Planetary Motion and were influential in getting Europe to accept the Copernican view of the universe. His horoscope is of special interest to Mercury students because it combines the best of Mercury efficiency with the worst of Mercury's byproducts: as a child, Brahe was abducted by a wealthy and childless uncle.

The factor that dominates Brahe's map is the strong eastern hemisphere. An emphasis in this portion of the chart gives privacy, introspection and sometimes narcissism. The placements of Capricorn, Aquarius and Virgo are significant. Not only does Saturn rule the ascendant and the Sun but its conjunction to Mercury in the eleventh house identifies him as having been remarkably efficient. The Moon's position with Uranus in Virgo shows an innovative quality: Brahe's contribution was to 'invent' a system that was unique to his taste. Neptune's relatively obscure placement probably accounts for his role as observer and technician.

Flexibility

Flexibility is Mercury's namesake, the cue card for keeping life loose, open and tentative. It is also Mercury's cure for cerebral lockjaw: as long as one can remain elastic, there is no danger of premature fossilization. The ideal proportion of flexibility in an individual is that amount which allows sufficient freedom for lateral thinking but not so much that the character becomes reduced to an amoebic mass — Mercury wants to be limber, not a jellyfish! Several horoscope features aid Mercury in its task. Mutables by sign or house introduce flexibility, other neutral planets (the Moon, Jupiter and Neptune) sustain it, and differentiation in the aspect structure offers it. The greater the number of 'patterns' in a map, the higher the number of alternatives. Whether flexibility is an asset or a distinct liability will depend on the overall structure of the chart: the final judgement rests with its relative coherence. Weak, unfocused aspect patterns merely reinforce the negative attributes of excessive mutability: the subject is unable to operate independently, is overly impressionable and lacking in will: external discipline thus becomes a necessity. Rigidity can have the reverse effect: an emphasis on the fixed signs, intercepted signs and low

point oppositions hems Mercury in. While interactable Mercury
is problematic, it is the malleable Mercury which breeds real
difficulty.

Too much flexibility minus any control imposed by strength in
the aspects, ego structure or planets invites an indiscriminate
association with an alleged 'authority' outside the self. Because
Mercury is inherently rebellious, especially active in youth and,
when over-emphasized, drawn to unreliable leaders, its influence
is seen to be particularly relevant in cases of delinquency and peer-
pressure behaviour of all kinds. Mercury adopts whatever value-
system it encounters. The outcome can be somewhat unfortunate,
as we shall see from the following example.

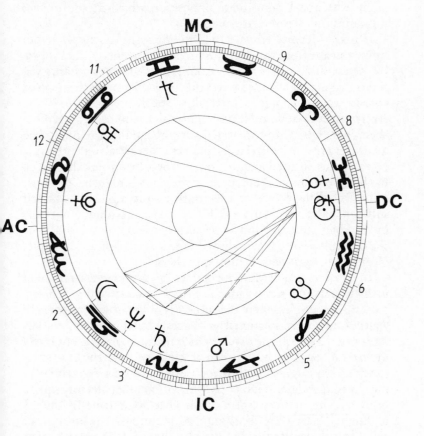

Figure 42   The horoscope chart of Patty Hearst.

Patty Hearst's chart is a superb example of the way a weak aspect structure in combination with pronounced mutability can in adolescence provoke serious difficulty. Hearst's chart suggests a rebellious conformist who is exaggeratedly responsive to whatever claims the world presents her with. She is the social chameleon who defines her colour by the company she keeps. The linear formation across the base of the chart indicates a tension between her ideological bias, which is clearly egalitarian, and the facts of her extreme socio-economic privilege. Hearst's need to be accepted by her peers, coupled with the diffused ego pattern, shows that she would be prime material for a decoy. Her victim/manipulator theme is emphasized by strong seventh house Pisces placements, along with the Uranus-node opposition which in adolescence promotes troublesome associates.

Hearst's Mercury vibrates to a 'rolling stone' atmosphere but cannot escape from the deeply entrenched parental values shown by the emphasis below the horizon: Hearst's secret militancy was thus a magnet for outside sources that could play on her unresolved conflict regarding material inequality. The Symbionese Liberation Army gladly seized on Hearst's ambivalence in order to achieve their own ends. Unfortunately its members, like Hearst, lacked a sufficient reality base. (Hearst projected her social injustice issues as well as her diffused identity: one can only bring back that which has been sent out, and of necessity, she would only attract an even more imbalanced case of the conflict from which she herself suffered.) Mercury's vulnerability is thus compounded not only by the chart structure and its seventh house position but also by the fact that it is organized through the Moon's contact principle: Hearst must find herself through others.

The final condition which marks Mercury as supremely important in this chart is its position within a separate aspect structure. Separate patterns, especially where the subject is in a state of comparative youth, function in isolation from the rest of their personality; they represent a niche in the psyche which is always present but rarely in control. Such structures can in time become the thread of considerable originality, but in youth they are responsible for unstable expression. It is especially significant that Mercury square Jupiter is the tightest aspect in the chart. The trine to Uranus highlights Hearst's publishing background — including her collaboration on her autobiography — as well as the high profile she attained within legal circles.

We have seen how Patty Hearst's intrinsic flexibility caused her

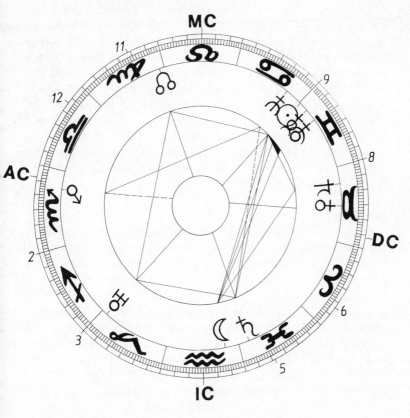

Figure 43   The horoscope chart of Jean-Paul Sartre.

grave problems. Adaptability can apply a different sort of pressure when trapped inside a fixed environment. Jean-Paul Sartre's exquisitely agile, albeit disciplined Mercury exemplifies Mercury stretched to its breaking point. Sartre's four-sided structure contains an envelope formation whcih the Hubers call a 'righteousness' figure. The key to the interpretation of this structure is that surface appearance disguises inner states. Aspects which shape the outside structure (trines and sextiles) evoke a calm, poised aspect, whereas the oppositions manifest conflict. The fact that the ego planets are also loosely connected suggests that the subject's air of coping very well in the world is a form of camouflage for emotional insularity. Fortunately, because Sartre is a writer, he actually presents these riddles to his readers.

Eight of the ten bodies are found in the west — Sartre, like Helen Keller, found other people vital to his sense of identity — yet the paradox of western horoscopes is that the need for others includes an element of hostility towards the condition of dependency. Sartre expresses this dilemma in the closing line of his play *No Exit: 'Hell is other people'*. [5] The Sun's Gemini location in close proximity to Mercury Pluto assures that the mind will dominate Mercury: Mercury will function almost exclusively in an intellectual mode. Sartre's modern attitudes are readily found in the Mercury-Pluto-Uranus aspect. The very title *No Exit* surely epitomizes Mercury's desperate claustrophobia in the eighth house grovelling for ninth house exposure.

Retrograde Mercury

Certain astrologers have observed that Mercury retrograde endows the subject with the ability to see through verbiage [7] and with the tendency to learn old lessons over and over again. [8] Unfortunately, I find no appreciable distinction between Mercury's direct or retrograde condition in natal charts. This is not to suggest that there are none but rather that, if they are present, such differences are markedly subtle, if not imperceptible. It would seem logical that some qualitative differences should occur, particularly in the light of the fact that Mercury progressions show specific shifts in their attitude and mode of being when the planet changes direction. If a qualitative distinction does exist, then I would follow Hebel's conclusion that Mercury retrograde types operate beneath the surface: they are naturally more intuitive, if not inclined to being more reticent, less forthright and marginally more reserved about expressing themselves. Sakoian claims that Cardinal Mercury makes a series of false starts and shows poor organizing skills, fixed Mercury seems incapable of acquiring the information necessary for the fulfilment of tasks and mutable Mercury RX increases indecision and vacillation. These observations make sense, but I myself have reached no definite conclusions about the actual difference.

Mercury transits certainly respond to textbook keywords: delays, commuter chaos, hold-ups in decision making, faulty communication by mail, telephone, etc., but these would seem relevant mainly to the charts of Mercury-ruled individuals and Mercury-connected businesses. A stationary Mercury is most emphatically influential in the natal horoscope, independent of the direction in which Mercury is moving, the key factor here being whether the change it indicates is to occur in the future — that is, within the first two years of life — or occurred before birth. The applying stationary motion is the most critical as it casts a somewhat anxious shadow over any action that Mercury undertakes, which is of course, coloured by the specific aspects and structure that Mercury inhabits.

Progressions

The chief principle to be adopted when interpreting progressions is that nothing should be read that is beyond the parameters of the natal horoscope; just as an accurate appraisal of Mercury requires a full delineation of the platform on which it rests, a progressed Mercury cannot be properly judged without an awareness of the natal chart's basic themes. The highly structured Saturn-ruled Mercury will find it rather uncomfortable when progressed Mercury entertains innovative action: instinctively, Saturn's Mercury withdraws. By contrast, the linear horoscope with a Moon-dominated Mercury will be excited — probably over-stimulated — by new ideas: this Mercury acts precipitously. The first Mercury hums and haws out of fear while the second rushes in enthusiastically, only to discover a comedy of errors. The cumulative effect in both cases is thus zero. Because Mercury is the main filtering device through which the ego functions, shifts of any nature affect the entire organism. Astrologically, these might involve the following: Mercury's change of direction from direct to retrograde motion and vice versa; a change of sign; and aspects to planets and house rulers, especially of AC-MC and the third and sixth houses. Mercury's progressions may or may not be compatible with the natal/progressed picture. The extent to which harmony and conflict exist between Mercury's working plan and the ego (other planets) agenda becomes the critical factor during moments of transition.

When Mercury changes course, communication enters a 'fog phase' of roughly three years. The applying stationary period, which lasts anything from one to two years usually brings a complete impasse; life enters a position of deadlock. The period of separation represents a trial time when the individual is still doubting, still unconvinced that he or she has taken the right decision. The post-direction period is one of building trust a gradual acceptance or understanding of new priorities. Age plays a crucial part in interpreting fog phases. Whatever has been learnt to date in terms of perception and means of expression no longer works. For the pre-school child just learning the alphabet, this can be quite disconcerting; the child might react by showing either a marked improvement or a decline in school performance. Mercury's new bearing has an equally unsettling effect on middle-aged or elderly people whose lives function in circumscribed ways: here the advent of Mercury's about-face is tantamount to a crisis. For the undisciplined, childlike personality or conversely the highly rigid, authoritarian one, Mercury's new thrust is similarly unnerving. The impact is typically confusion, indecision — a state of limbo. The action-motivated temperament is the one most peeved by this limbo, and yet, during Mercury's 'fog phase', the best strategy is calculated waiting, deliberately treading water. By consciously accepting the condition rather than fighting it, one minimizes the distress signals and saves a lot of wasted energy. Drowning occurs more often than not from exhaustion: flapping about in the water only accentuates the danger of going under. The most common form of flapping about is negative thinking. However much constructive action has been taken in order to change undesirable conditions, the fog state clouds any genuine awareness of progress. Individuals need a few years in their new framework in order to be thoroughly convinced that a metamorphosis has indeed taken place. (This attitude is by no means limited to Mercury progressions!)

In consultation, one frequently sees people whose lives have been assaulted by numerous ups and downs over stretches of ten to fifteen years. While I as an astrologer know that each individual is responsible for his or her destiny and that the esoteric perspective dictates that each person gets precisely what he or she deserves, such statements are of no help to the person at the end of his tether. Consider the fatigue and exhaustion one might feel after that much frustration. As astrologers, we know that change comes, that each of us has some role in shaping our lives; we also know that certain cycles are more tedious than others. To pretend otherwise is astrological claptrap. I cannot expect clients to *believe* me when I state that a better cycle is around the corner; their experience refutes that probability. They may hope I am right, even trust me when I say that it is possible, but they won't believe it until some time has passed and they are able to look back over their shoulder and see that yes, after year such and such the trend really did shift upwards. The same principle applies to Mercury progressions. Individuals must be encouraged to bide their time, have patience and allow the process to announce moments of appropriate action. Turning inwards during 'fogs' alleviates any danger of serious imbalance. Clients must be reassured that feedback from the environment might not be immediately satisfactory or even forthcoming. Post-Mercury directional changes works like blind man's buff: one agrees to take risks in the dark, without any guarantee of when or if anything productive will come of it. Tentative, gentle steps are the safest.

While the stationary period is characterized by regressive behaviour, qualitative distinctions exist between Mercury's retrograde and direct types of motion. These are further refined by the factors of gender and masculine/feminine consciousness.

MERCURY **DIRECT**	**Retrograde:** A feeling of backing up, of retreading familiar ground. A shift to an introspective slant. Tendency to renege on previous views. A return to earlier or dormant interests. A breakthrough to the emotional, inner world. A subjective bias. *Masculine:* A natural resistance to the condition. A tendency to react by moodiness, psychosomatic illness. *Feminine:* Absorbs the process more easily. The condition awakens the imaginative, contemplative side.
MERCURY **RETROGRADE**	**Direct:** A sense of moving forward. The attitude adopted is more logical, systematic. The holding patterns are lifted. A breakthrough to the outer world: new starts, important decision making. *Masculine:* A sense of relief. A marked shift in confidence: assertiveness increases. *Feminine:* An ambivalent entry to the outer realm. A difficult transition into 'masculine' consciousness. An initially aggressive, noisy passage. This gradually tapers off as the perspective is digested by the psyche.

Note:
Obviously, a male can have an essentially feminine consciousness and a female an essentially masculine consciousness, in which case their respective reactions to the conditions outlined above would be more complex.

Table 10   The effects of direct/retrograde motion

Several of our chart examples had Mercury switch direction during their lifetime. Alexander Graham Bell's Mercury assumed retrograde motion when he was twenty years old. His biographer quotes a letter from his mother received on his twentieth birthday which expressed concern about his personal ill-health. The letter advised him that she was sending 'a little Mercurius for bile'. [9] During this time, Bell complained that he was unable to decide whether he was mentally or physically depressed. Also significant during Bell's Mercury progression was the loss of his younger brother, Ted. Bell's siblings (described by the third house ruler, Mercury, situated in Pisces would be prone to lung-related disease. In fact, both of Bell's brothers died of tuberculosis; the first, however, died during the retrograde motion phase. When Mercury retrograded back to the conjunction with Uranus, the older brother died and Bell set sail for America. Synastry buffs will note that Bell's Jupiter in 8° Gemini conjoins the USA's ascendant and Uranus: Bell's new-found independence equally brought a new kind of freedom to the American people. Later, at age 45, Mercury's direct motion prompted Bell to fund the American Association of Promotion of Teaching Speech to the Deaf, which still serves its founder's aims.

Helen Keller's stationary retrograde period occurred just at the time when her tutor-companion, Barbara Sullivan, was married. For Helen this meant a considerable rearrangement of life style. Initially, she used this time for cultivating her senses, for experiencing greater solitude. Later, when she was about fifty, Mercury's direct motion accompanied the expansion of her raising activities.

Patty Hearst's chart illustrates the problems caused by Mercury's changing direction during the subject's formative years. Here Mercury is not only the chart ruler but is also placed in the extremely pliable sign of Pisces in that conformist and manipulative niche, the seventh house. Mercury stationary direct coincided with her two-year involvement with the Symbionese Liberation Army. At twenty-one, when Mercury moved direct, she was captured by the FBI. Notice how in her case Mercury's rulership of the ascendant and midheaven resulted in major life complications when its progressions occurred: Hearst's reputation and freedom of movement suffered due to her imprisonment. In Bell's case, his first house Mercury in Pisces ruling the third and seventh houses shows that progressions would have a direct impact on him (ascendant-first house) but also that these would be connected with a sibling or partner.

Change of Sign

The minute Mercury moves from one sign to the next, priorities change. This entry into a new element introduces a 'different' reality, one which may be wholly or only partially assimilated. This atmosphere may either be at complete variance with Mercury's known territory or altogether familiar to it. Progressions by sign are like plastic overlays superimposed on original documents: the natal themes remain intact, but are infused with alternative viewpoints derived from the sign's element. Since Mercury can travel through up to five signs in a ninety-year human lifespan, the way to observe its long-range development is to consider the elemental sequence. The starting point is Mercury's natal position. The element the planet tenants there governs the sequence it will follow:

Fire sequence:	FIRE → EARTH → AIR → WATER
Earth sequence:	EARTH → AIR → WATER → FIRE
Air sequence:	AIR → WATER → FIRE → EARTH
Water sequence:	WATER → FIRE → EARTH → AIR

The sequence above illustrates several features worth noting in connection with Mercury's element progression:

1. Jungian astrologers will note that natal Mercury direct in fire and air have an early contact with their psychological opposite. (fire / earth, air / water), whereas natal Mercury direct in water and earth have to postpone contact with their psychological opposite until the very last stage of their development (water / air, earth / fire). This condition is obviously reversed if Mercury's natal position is retrograde. One might infer tentatively that fire and air signs, in keeping with their positive valence, develop more rapidly when motion is direct. Similarly, it would appear that water and earth signs benefit considerably — and have their negative valence offset — by having natal positions that are retrograde.

2. Mercury's long-term objectives (represented by the element furthest from the natal placement) are not always connected to its psychological opposite, thus:

Natal fire	must acquire water's humility, compassion.
Natal earth	must acquire fire's spiritual independence.
Natal air	must acquire earth's physical duty.
Natal water	must acquire air's logical intellect.

Again one might conclude, cautiously, that the positive signs (fire and air) conquer their psychological opposite more easily than do the negative signs (water and earth).

Aspects to Planets and House Rulers

Progressed Mercury aspects to planets call for the same procedure that applies to a consideration of the natal picture: the aspects are always judged within the context of the horoscope as a whole. If the astrologer has some knowledge of the individual's personal threshold for pain, stress and adaptability, the probable outcome of progression factors will be easier to ascertain. A progressed Mercury that means entering the influence of Mars will have a very different impact on someone who is placid and self-effacing by nature than it will on the native Martian personality. Similarly, a highly Uranian disposition will find the Mercury-Saturn aspect a mite claustrophobic. Gender consciousness may also influence the person's reactions to certain inner changes marked by Mercury progressions. For example, someone with a strongly rational masculine consciousness may feel somewhat uncomfortable when his or her Mercury interacts with Neptune, while a receptive, intuitive feminine consciousness may feel quite at home with the same aspect.

Look for a sympathy or an antipathy between the mental attitude suggested by the natal Mercury and the world-view of the progressed Mercury; the type of aspect that Mercury makes to other planets is less important. Hard aspects are much more conspicuous in terms of the opportunity for change. Soft aspects, on the other hand, may simply introduce new ideas to a flow of development which had already been set in motion. Count on the hard ones for indications of abrupt changes in thought and behaviour (see pages 187-9). Pay particular attention to Mercury progressions to those houses and rulers which affect over-all well-being whether physical or psychological. In specific, rulers and planets of the AC, MC, 3rd and 6th houses are especially relevant to an assessment of attitudes and circumstances that might trigger psychosomatic illness.

Mercury governs thinking and is therefore directly linked to health imbalances which arise out of negative thought process. Chronic fatigue, when there is no other explanation for it, is a good index that Mercury's right functioning is askew. This is often a signal that the working environment is unsatisfactory or that the individual is somehow unable to express his or her real views about a situation. Communication inhibition, for whatever reasons, is one of Mercury's more obvious symptoms of malaise.

Posthumous Progressions

One of astrology's great mysteries is the way that progressions and transits operate posthumously. The fact that these continue to function in accordance with the laws of astrology suggests that this field clearly draws no distinction between physical and spiritual existence: in astrology, life is eternal. The following example offers a clear demonstration of the effects of a posthumous progression. Public interest in that nineteenth-century physical freak, the Elephant Man[10] (Joseph Merrick) and his doctor ally Sir Frederick Treves revived in 1977, when a play and film were made about their relationship. *The Elephant Man*'s huge critical and popular success is symbolically etched in the progressions that took place in that year in the charts of both individuals. The fact that Treves taught Merrick to both speak and write suggests that Mercury ties should be evident not only synastrically but in the later progressions which signalled the date of the retelling of their story.

Firstly, however, we cannot afford to ignore Frederick Treves's natal Saturn in conjunction with Merrick's Pluto (which squares his Sun). The time of the play's opening brought his Uranus (in

JOSEPH MERRICK	FREDERICK TREVES
Sun 12 Leo 44	Sun 26 Aquarius 47
Moon 13 Sagittarius 10	Moon 19 Taurus 56
Mercury 28 Cancer 26	Mercury 18 Aquarius 14
Venus 10 Cancer 56	Venus 4 Aquarius 43
Mars 14 Aries 3	Mars 22 Aquarius 21
Jupiter 26 Virgo 11	Jupiter 20 Sagittarius 12
Saturn 20 Virgo 36	Saturn 12 Taurus 06
Uranus 19 Gemini 34	Uranus 4 Taurus 58
Neptune 3 Aries 39	Neptune 0 Pisces 37
Pluto 11 Taurus 10	Pluto 29 Aries 45
PROGRESSIONS TO 1977	
Sun 9 Sagittarius 05	Sun 0 Cancer 54
Mercury 27 Scorpio 23	Mercury 11 Cancer 25
Saturn 3 Libra 49	Uranus 11 Taurus 17
	Saturn 26 Taurus 22

Joseph Merrick: August 5, 1862 Leicester.
Frederick Treves: February 15, 1853 London assumed.

Table 11 Noon positions for the horoscope of Joseph Merrick and Frederick Treves.

11° Taurus) into precise conjunction with his friend's Pluto. Merrick's progressed Mercury at 27 degrees of Scorpio applied by trine to his own Mercury at 28 degrees of Cancer which reinforced his singular Mercury natal aspect, sextile to Jupiter: the advent of this progressed Mercury rekindled the public's awareness of Merrick's plight. Frederick Treves's Mercury has progressed to a conjunction with progressed Venus at 11° Cancer, both of which form a sextile to the progressed Uranus at 11° Taurus and which, very recently became separated from its conjunction with Merrick's 11° Cancer Venus. The themes raised in all the media reviews of *The Elephant Man* were those of love and deep respect.

Next, we should recall that Treves's work with Merrick entailed an enormous amount of patience. Notice that his Pluto at 29° Aries forms a tight square to Merrick's Mercury: Treves raised his friend up from a state of real despair. Their mutual admiration and interest in communication shows in Treves's 18° Aquarius Mercury, which trines and forms a mutual reception with Merrick's Uranus position.

Mutual Reception
Planets in mutual reception occupy the signs of one another's respective rulership or dignity: for example, Mercury in Leo mutually receives the Sun in Virgo. The exchange of power between two planets in mutual reception is allegedly beneficial and strengthening. Because Mercury rules both Gemini and Virgo the

SIGN POSITION OF MERCURY	PLANET IN MERCURY'S SIGN
Aries	Mars: Gemini or Virgo
Taurus	Venus: Gemini
Gemini	Mercury's own sign
Cancer	Moon: Gemini or Virgo
Leo	Sun: Gemini (late) or Virgo
Virgo	Mercury's own sign
Libra	Venus: Virgo
Scorpio	Pluto: Gemini or Virgo
Sagittarius	Jupiter: Gemini or Virgo
Capricorn	Saturn: Gemini or Virgo
Aquarius	Uranus: Gemini or Virgo
Pisces	Neptune: Gemini or Virgo

Table 12   Mutual reception table for Mercury.

condition is not uncommon. Mutual reception by degree is a horary refinement which gives added flexibility to planetary options. Mercury is thus allowed extra leeway for making quick exits, for changing its spots. Mutual reception placements are conceivably those planets in the chart with maximum free will. They certainly enhance a structure that is already powerful and suggest means of tightening one that lacks either symmetry or cohesion. Although horary experts generally frown on the use of horary techniques in natal astrology, I personally have found mutual reception by degree to be very illuminating in birth charts, especially when the exchange by degree introduces new aspects. Mercury is definitely responsive to mutual reception escape clauses: it enjoys the built-in advantage of choice.

Mercury Aspects
Hard aspects: (Conjunction, Opposition, Semi-square, Sesquiquadrate and Quincunx.)
Soft aspects: (Trine, Sextile, Semi-sextile.)

Hard versus Soft Aspects
While traditional astrology interpreted hard aspects as being difficult or onerous and soft aspects as being easy or fortuitous, today's mainstream astrologer reverses this ethic. It is the trines and sextiles which bear the astrologer's animosity. Even psychological astrologers exhibit preference for those aspects which promote rather than deter change. Modern astrologers praise the problem-solving hard aspects and pooh-pooh the *mananna* type soft aspects. I suspect the reason for this interpretive about-face arises from the fundamental shift in the socio-economic status of astrologers. Recall that historically astrologers only served the privileged classes. Astrologers were among the educated elite themselves. Not surprisingly, those astrological factors which preserved the status quo (i.e. trines) acquired special significance. The notion of 'luck' or 'good fortune' is now superseded by the idea of 'luck' arising from direct effort (i.e. squares). Astrologers no longer occupy the social elite. Nor do the bulk of their clients. Astrologers and their patrons consist of the socially mobile commercial classes. Those aspects which reinforce the overall mood of society will naturally be more highly prized. Note that Hindu astrology still retains a negative attitude toward oppositions and squares, which of course reflects the comparatively static, tradition-bound society in which it functions. Clearly, if a society perceives

change as its greatest threat, then that society's astrologers will see hard aspects as its biggest burden.

For our purposes, hard aspects simply *force* expression of planetary energy whereas soft aspects *allow* expression of planetary energy. Hard aspects are more compulsive in their operation; soft aspects are less driven in their operation. Hard aspects to Mercury mean an analytical, discriminating mode of expression, while soft aspects imply an intuitive, spontaneous one.

Hard Aspects

A *Conjunction* maximizes Mercury's sign quality: the tighter the conjunction the more difficult it is to differentiate between this planet and its partner. The aspecting planet assumes complete control of the Mercury function. This is particularly evident in the case of the Sun. Isolated conjunctions of Mercury increase freedom but diminish reliability: a classic example of this would be a conversation comprised of *non sequiturs*.

The Opposition is dialogue-orientated; Mercury in opposition loves debate. There is a tendency to instruct, proselytize. The temperament may be quite argumentative as well as fond of theory. This see-saw effect may result in personal indecisiveness. An opposition can also trigger the projection of attitudes and beliefs onto other individuals.

The *Square* is accomplishment-orientated. The subject's expression may be harsh and deliberate. Squares tend to tighten or abbreviate communication. Aspects to Mercury have a hacksaw or scalpel effect. The filtering system is keen. The ability to analyse may be an asset or a deficit: critical faculties can be best employed either in writing or editorial work.

Semisquares and *Sesquiquadrates* share the square's priority of achievement but sharpen the perception at the expense of a considerable degree of nervous tension. They suggest fits of brilliance, hair-splitting. *Semisquares* show a more direct, practical style of communication: associate these with the struggle for growth, labour pains, getting things off the ground. *Sesquiquadrates* veer towards the creative, intellectual mode. The fluttery irritability is more likely to be the result of self-generated problems than is the annoyance displayed by semi-squares, whose frustration is more obviously located in first efforts. The sesquiquadrate shows an element of perfectionism, an inability to let go of material until it is absolutely satisfactory.

Quincunxes are consciousness raisers and have a surrealistic side: they are provocative and catalytic. Quincunxes to Mercury force some modification of the thinking process, which is often accompanied by a health crisis. Its originality of expression is high, assuming that the environment is low attention span. Body co-ordination poor. Timing and rhythm off. Subject's management of a Mercury quincunx improves with age.

Trines are magnetic, flowing aspects suggesting fluent, spontaneous expression and thinking that is unedited, possibly naïve. Their rhetoric is artful, rhetorical: evangelical leaders usually have these persuasive, soft-sell aspects present in their charts. The impact is subtle, effortless. Trines are also characteristic of musical ability and artistic appreciation.

Sextiles are aspects that suggest a practical, efficient, logical mode of expression. They possess natural integrative faculties, their approach being reasonable, co-operative and systematic.

Semi-sextiles are information processors. These Mercury aspects are particularly finely tuned and intuitive. Environmental sensors or detectors, semi-sextiles pick up vibrations very quickly. These aspects usually require special training or development in order to be fully utilized. Also common to Mercury semi-sextiles is the ability to listen with the 'inner mind' or 'third ear'. Like quincunxes, the semi-sextile benefits by the process of maturity.

Unaspected Mercury

Mercury unaspected calls for a careful assessment of the relative symmetry of the aspect-structure, ego strength and bias. If the horoscope features closely knit aspects, then Mercury's condition will depict precocity, wit and an acceptable 'trickster'. However, if the self-esteem lacks fibre and the aspects bounce around inexplicably without any clear focus, Mercury may evoke the irrepressible juvenile whose constant need for attention exasperates both friend and foe. Mercury unaspected can be one of the freest, most creative of minds; the important thing is that it must *invent* a means of co-operating with the rest of the chart. This also necessitates staying power. Fixed signs and a reasonable Saturn influence can help to stabilize excessive mutability. A deliberate bonding with one or more planetary allies gives Mercury exceptional virtuosity.

Weak Aspects to Mercury

Far more difficult than unaspected Mercury is the situation whereby few contacts are made to the planet and those that do exist are very wide in orb. The communication signals are faint, coming in and going out. Psychologically, this can be one of the most frustrating in the worldly sense because all efforts to offset it are undermined. The weak aspect *is* transmitting something, though it is merely a whisper. Unless there is an alliance with a powerful ego structure, the chances are that the individual will prefer to remain silent or unacknowledged by the world. The main problem arises from insecurity about what it is that one has to contribute and an inability to code it properly. The timid, anxious ego benefits from a protective climate in which its faint murmurs receive full attention.

Mercury-Pluto: Secretive. Insight, perspective. Privately rebellious. School truants. Manipulates by silence. Obsessional; fanatical intensity. A belief in an unseen authority. Motivated by power or the pull of the mysteries. Action is premeditated. Powerful observational skills; natural sleuths. Tyranny of the word. A resistance to closed systems: for females this can manifest as block when it comes to maths. A need to penetrate the unknown for the purpose of control. A black, sadistic sense of humour. A human lie-detector. A wilful style of expression and a lethal tongue. A paralytic stare. Stiff movement; tense gestures. A precocious sexuality.

Mercury-Neptune: Visionary. A purveyor of myths, fairy tales. Musical ability. Forgetful, inattentive at school. Natural mediators. Superb strategists. Master image-makers in the realms of photography, the cinema and poetry. Their mental elasticity includes a capacity to master foreign language sounds easily. An acquisition of knowledge by osmosis. A good ear for sound (music and accent). Naturally evasive, but not for the same reasons as Mercury-Pluto: the need here is for fantasy, mystery. An affinity with nature, animals. Childhood experience of abandonment: a feeling of being orphaned. Siblings often missing, may be substituted for by imaginary playmates. Charming, charismatic speakers. Highly seductive *and* easily seduced. Fluid, graceful movement. Excellent dancers.

Mercury-Uranus: Extra-sensory perception. A restless, impatient disposition. An inquisitive and acquisitive mind, original and inventive. A lover of the avant-garde. A logical, systematic mind that often jumps steps in the process of explaining to others. A low opinion of authority. A caustic tongue. A spontaneous, perverse sense of humour. In a group, this person's behaviour is often disruptive, catalytic. Surrogate mother-figures such as a grandmother or grandfather, nannies, aunts, etc., play a significant role in the person's development. Unusual siblings, and a detached, erratic relationship with them. Abrupt; the speech is lightning fast. Computer wizards; mechanical tinkerers.

Mercury-Saturn: Authoritative, scientific, mathematical and scholarly; obliged to teach or to set examples for others. Communication is often inhibited, due to a variety of tactics; a tendency to ask unanswerable or rhetorical questions. The audience recognizes the intelligence of authority of the individual but is left speechless or incapable of responding to them. The tone or sound of the voice conveys a vast scholarship, and the person's intellectual power is inclined to inhibit less articulate individuals. A tendency to be pedantic; a nit-picker. Mercury-Saturn controls by the sound of the voice. The mother's influence on formal or informal education is very important; if the mother did not value learning, its opposites may result: isolation, depression and inhibited speech. Oral compulsions include talking, smoking and eating. A fear of rejection by the mother (Saturn) and later by society breeds a complacent, conformist temperament that hides its needs through such things as compulsive talking, smoking and eating. A perfectionist. Siblings are treated as children or at arm's length; often geographically separated from them.

Mercury-Jupiter: Conveys a philosophical slant, a stress on breadth of experience, knowledge of life. A religious orientation. Optimistic. Natural orators, lecturers, proselytizers. A need to travel both physically and mentally. A tendency to generalize, make sweeping statements, attuned to moral and ethical issues; a legal mind. Attuned to the spirit of the law rather than the letter of the law. May slip into prejudice and heavy, judgemental moralizing if not careful; may pontificate now and then. Careless and slapdash about details; 'absent-minded professor' types. Humorous, high-spirited. Gestures are broad and open; the subject may bump into things, as he or she tends to be looking much further away than the immediate surroundings. Sibling's involvement generous and infrequent.

Mercury-Mars: A quick, razor-edged mentality; a logical, practical turn of mind disposed toward mathematics, science and medicine. A natural debater, alert, competitive and aggressive. Tendency toward sarcasm, satire. Speech quick, blunt, punctuated, abrupt. Can define a bully. Strong intellectual/physical bond with siblings. Precision of movement. Word wizards. Athletic.

Mercury-Venus: Diplomatic communication. A strong practical or business sense. An appreciation of beauty. Literary abilities if Moon and Neptune also strong. Sentimental. Co-operative, pleasing. A strong sense of protocol and etiquette. Mathematical abilities related to form, conceptualization. Passive, affectionate ties to siblings.

Mercury-Moon: Natural common sense. An excellent memory. An alert mind; an interest in current affairs makes them fine journalists. Skilled at neutral observation. Public-minded. High sensitivity, often accompanied by extremely high intelligence.

Mercury-Sun: Logical consistency. High regard for intellect. Warmth and vitality of expression. Preoccupation with the self as shown by continual use of 1st person singular 'I'. Tendency for being dogmatic.

Notes
1. Josephine Tey, *The Man in the Queue* (Peter Davies, London, 1927) p.138.
2. Bruno and Louise Huber, *Man and His World* (Weiser, 1979). Pivotal influence in my own work as an astrologer. While the Hubers do not assign Mercury the same significance I attach to it, it has been through their principles philosophy that I've come to know a great deal more about the Mercury type.
3. The Hubers identity aspects by colour notation. Type A Conjunction, Opposition, Square — Red, Type B Trine, Sextile —Blue; and Type C, Semi-sextile and Quincunx — Green.
4. Ego strength is my term for the relative integration of the Hubers' three ego planets: the Sun, the Moon and Saturn. This has an important bearing on the individual's stress capacity as well as the orientation, whether mental, emotional or physical. Ego strength influences Mercury's behaviour in the same way one would expect that a ship's hull or structure (Saturn), the fluctuating waves/weather (Moon) and the captain's intelligence (Sun) would affect routine sailing (Mercury). The crisis of one element taxes the resources of the

Bias: Vertical/hierarchical   Horizontal/egalitarian   Triangular/creative
      Linear/mental   Rectangular/pragmatic

Gender: Masculine/Feminine   Hemisphere: Northern/Subjective   Eastern/Self
                                          Southern/Objective   Western/Others

Motivation: Aspect Structure Coherent/Strong
            Aspect Structure Loose/Weak

Ego Strength: Sun/Mental   Moon/Emotional   Saturn/Physical

Aspect Types: A   B   C   F   A   W   E

Sign Emphasis: F   A   W   E   Environmental Supports: C   F   M

Mercury Considerations: Conclusions:

Angularity   Dominance + –   Dominance ±
Closest Aspect   Efficiency
Number of Aspects   Flexibility
Gemini/Virgo Emphasis   Originality
Degree Strength   Hermes
Mutual Reception   Thoth
House, Sign, Dispositor
Rulership, Detriment, Exaltation, Fall

Defence choices:

Rationalization   v   Objectivity
Projection   v   Empathy
Denial/Repression v   Substitution/Sublimation

Mercury Checklist

	MERCURY STRONG	MERCURY WEAK
SATURN (Physical world)	Mechanical skills, realm of applied sciences, high agility, engineering, mathematics, dexterity clerical abilities, high detail.	Unskilled, skilled labour support staff, maintenance crews Low detail work.
MOON (Emotional world)	Helping professions, Nursing, public relations, teaching, lower level therapeutic jobs, sales, advertising. insurance.	Back up support staff people Service personnel, domestic service, receptionists, child care. Low pressure sales.
SUN (Mental world)	Leadership roles, executive skills. Creativity and theoretical abilities. Teaching at professional levels. Positions of autonomy and independence. Capacity for abstraction very high.	Mind wants to work, lead, but can't seem to express itself Benefits most by arduous discipline and careful education.

Table 13   The combined effects of Mercury and the ego planets.

other. Mercury 'breaks down' when it senses the ego planets, combined strengths and unduly burdened.

5. Ralph Harrity and G. Martin, *Three Lives of Helen Keller* (Hodder & Stoughton, London, 1962) p.8. Biographical information attained here.

6. Jean-Paul Sartre, *No Exit* (Vantage Books, 1955).

7. Doris Hebel, *The Aquarian Agent*.

8. Frances Sakoian and L. Acker, *The Importance of Mercury in the Horoscope*, Copyright Frances Sakoian, 1970.

9. Robert V. Bruce, *Bell: Alexander Graham Bell and the Conquest of Solitude* (Little Brown, 1973) p.53.

10. Michael Howell and Peter Ford, *The True History of the Elephant Man* (Penguin, Harmondsworth, 1981).

Horoscope Data

Key to sources:

BIO   Autobiography/biography.

CIR   *Circle Book of Charts,* compiled by Stephen Erlewine, (American Publication, 1972).

DOD   Carolyn R. Dodson, *Horoscopes of the US States & Cities* (Copyright, 1975).

GAU   M. and F. Gauquelin, *Writers and Journalists,* Volume 6, (1970-1971).

LR   Lois M. Rodden, *Profiles of Women,* 1980. *The American Book of Charts* (Astro Computing Services, 1980).

NEWS   Newspaper articles/*Sunday Telegraph* information service.

PEN   Marc Penfield, *2001: The Penfield Collection,* 1979.

PRIV   Author files.

SPEC   Rectification/speculative time.

Friedrich Nietzsche: October 15, 1844. 10.00 a.m. LMT.
Rocken, Germany (LR).   70
Andy Warhol: October 28, 1930. Forest City, Pennsylvania
(BIO). Jean Stein and George Plimpton, *Edie: An
American Biography.* Photograph of Warhol's birth
certificate in book, but no time given.   74
Paul Klee: December 18, 1879. 4.00 a.m. LMT (Other
time: 10.45 a.m.). Munchenbuschee, Switzerland (LR).
Also Thomas Ring, Bruno Huber, Wangemann.   76
Sigmund Freud: May 6, 1856. 6.30 p.m. LMT. Frieberg,
Germany (LR).   93
John McEnroe: February 16, 1959. 9.30 p.m. GMT.
Wiesbaden, Germany. *Astrological Lodge Quarterly*
Spring, 1984.   94
Oscar Wilde: October 16, 1854, 3.00 a.m. LMT. Dubin,
Ireland. (LR).   96
Brooke Shields: May 31, 1965. 1.45 p.m. EDT, NYC,
New York (LR).   98
Cryonics Corporation: July 10, 1967, midnight.
Los Angeles, California (PRIV). Conversation with Dept. of
Corporations, State of California/Sacramento.
Suspension: February 1, 1971.   100
USA: July 4, 1776. 2.13 a.m. Philadelphia,
Pennsylvania. (DOD).   102
State of California: September 9, 1850. Noon. Acceptance
into Union (DOD).   104
Marquis de Sade: June 2, 1740. 9.13 p.m. LMT (SPEC)
(LR quotes 9.13 p.m. LMT, 7.15 a.m., 2.00 a.m.).   114
John Gacey: March 17, 1942. 00.20 a.m. CWT. Chicago,
Illinois (LR).   115
Alain Robbe-Grillet: August 18, 1922. 7.30 a.m. ST. Brest,
France (GAU).   119
Samaritans Organization: November 2, 1953. London
(BIO). Midnight chosen because it is the beginning
of the day.   128
Guardian Angels: February 13, 1979. Bronx, NYC,
New York. 1.30 p.m. EST (PRIV). From Guardian Angels'
leader Lisa Evers to author.   132
London: June 30, 1052. 3.07 a.m. (SPEC). Vivian Robson
did a rectification on this in *Astrology Quarterly* Vol. 14,
No. 4 (Dec 1940).   136
San Francisco: April 15, 1850. 8.27 a.m. First City
Charter (DOD).   139

Select Bibliography

Garth Allen, *Taking the Kid Gloves off Astrology* (Clancy Publications, 1975).

Patrick Boylan, *Thoth, Hermes of Egypt: A Study of Some Aspects of Theological Thought in Ancient Egypt* (Oxford University Press, 1922).

Norman O. Brown, *Hermes the Thief: The Evolution of a Myth* (University of Wisconsin Press, 1947).

R. T. Clark, Rundle, *Myth and Symbol in Ancient Egypt* (Thames and Hudson, London, 1978).

H. L. Cornell, *Dictionary of Medical Astrology* (Llewellyn Publications, St. Paul, Minnesota, 1973).

Geoffrey Dean, *Recent Advances in Natal Astrology: A Critical Review 1900-1976*, Astrological Association, 1977.

L. R. Farnell, *The Cults of Greek States V* (Oxford University Press, 1909).

Marie-Louise Von Franz, *Puer Aeternus* (Sigo Press, Santa Monica, 1981).

Robert Graves, *The Greek Myths* I & II, (Penguin Books, Harmondsworth, 1960 and 1972).

Adolf Guggen-Buhl-Craig, *Power in the Helping Professions* (Spring Publications, Zurich, 1976).

Bruno and Louise Huber, *Man and His World* (Samuel Weiser, New York, 1978).

C. G. Jung, *The Archetypes and the Collective Unconscious,* Collected Works Volume 9, 'On the Psychology of the Trickster Figure' (Bollingen Series XX, Princeton, 1975).

——, *Alchemical Studies,* 'The Spirit Mercurius', Collective Works Volume 13, (Routledge and Kegan Paul, London, 1968).

——, *Mysterium Coniunctionis,* Collected Works Volume 14 (Routledge and Kegan Paul, London, 1963).

Emma Jung, *Animus and Anima* (Spring Publications, Zurich, 1957).

Karl Kerenyi, *The Gods of the Greeks* (Thames and Hudson, London, 1976).

——, *Hermes: Guide of Souls* (Spring Publications, Zurich, 1976).

——, *The Heroes of the Greeks* (Thames and Hudson, London, 1978).

Kirk, G. S., *The Nature of Greek Myths* (Penguin Books, Harmondsworth, 1974).

Christopher Lasch, *The Culture of Narcissism* (Abacus, London, 1980).

Firmicus Maternus, *Ancient Astrology: Theory and Practice,* Noyes Classical Studies, 1975.

Lois M. Rodden, *The American Book of Charts* (Astro Computing Services, San Diego, 1980).

Frances Sakoian and L. Acker, *The Importance of Mercury in the Horoscope* (Sakoian and Acker, 1970).

Michael Simpson, *Gods and Heroes of the Greeks: The Library of Apollodorus* (University of Massachusetts, Boston, 1976).

June Singer, *Androgyny* (Anchor Press, New York, 1976).

J. Viau, *Egyptian Mythology* (Hamlyn Press, London, 1965).

John Wilson, *The Culture of Ancient Egypt* (University of Chicago, 1971).

Index